Greenland

Greenland

BY JEAN F. BLASHFIELD

Enchantment of the World
Second Series

Children's Press®

A Division of Scholastic Inc.

NEW YORK   TORONTO   LONDON   AUCKLAND   SYDNEY
MEXICO CITY   NEW DELHI   HONG KONG
DANBURY, CONNECTICUT

Frontispiece: Ilulissat Village

Consultant: Shawn Marshall, PhD, Department of Geography, University of Calgary, Calgary, Alberta, Canada

Please note: All statistics are as up-to-date as possible at the time of publication.

Book production by Herman Adler Design

Library of Congress Cataloging-in-Publication Data

Blashfield, Jean F.
  Greenland / by Jean F. Blashfield.
        p. cm. — (Enchantment of the world. Second series)
  Includes bibliographical references and index.
  ISBN 0-516-23678-4
  1. Greenland—Juvenile literature. I. Title. II. Series.
  G743.B43 2005
  998'.2—dc22   2005000755

CHILDREN'S PRESS and associated logos are trademarks and/or registered
trademarks of Scholastic Library Publishing. SCHOLASTIC and associated logos
are trademarks and/or registered trademarks of Scholastic Inc.
1 2 3 4 5 6 7 8 9 10 R 14 13 12 11 10 09 08 07 06 05

Greenland

Contents

Cover photo:
Young Green-
lander wearing
a fur-lined parka

CHAPTER

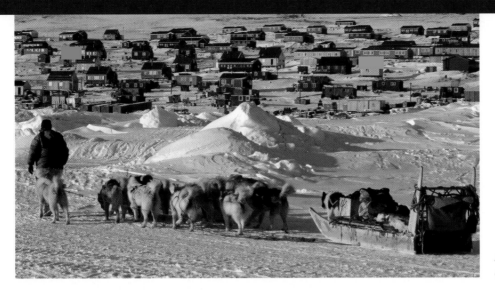

An Inuit hunter and his dog team

An Inuit wood carving

North of
Everywhere

8

GREENLAND IS THE WORLD'S LARGEST ISLAND. It stretches from the Arctic Ocean down to the North Atlantic. Despite its name, Greenland is green only around its southern edges. The rest of it is covered with ice.

The name *Greenland* was first used by Viking explorer Erik (or Eirik as it is spelled in the sagas) the Red in the tenth century. Perhaps he thought the image of a green land would cause people to follow him. Sixteenth-century English explorer John Davis had a different name for Greenland. He called it the Land of Desolation.

Most of Greenland is north of the Arctic Circle, an area often defined as any land that experiences twenty-four hours of darkness in the winter. No land is closer to the North Pole than northern Greenland. Because Greenland is so far north, it is completely dark for many weeks in the winter. The sun never rises then.

Opposite: **Aerial view of Nuussuaq Peninsula, Disko Bay, and West Greenland**

Erik the Red sets sail for Greenland.

Because the land is covered with a thick sheet of glacial ice, most of Greenland has never been explored. Snow that falls in the middle of the ice cap becomes buried and stays there for more than one hundred thousand years. Snow that falls near the edge of the ice cap melts during the summer or gets transported to the coast where it breaks off. This ice cap is so big that if it were to melt entirely, all the oceans of the world would rise 23 feet (7 meters). Parts of Greenland's glaciers are constantly breaking off and falling into the ocean. The sea surrounding the island churns with icebergs.

A fishing boat makes its way through glacial ice near West Greenland.

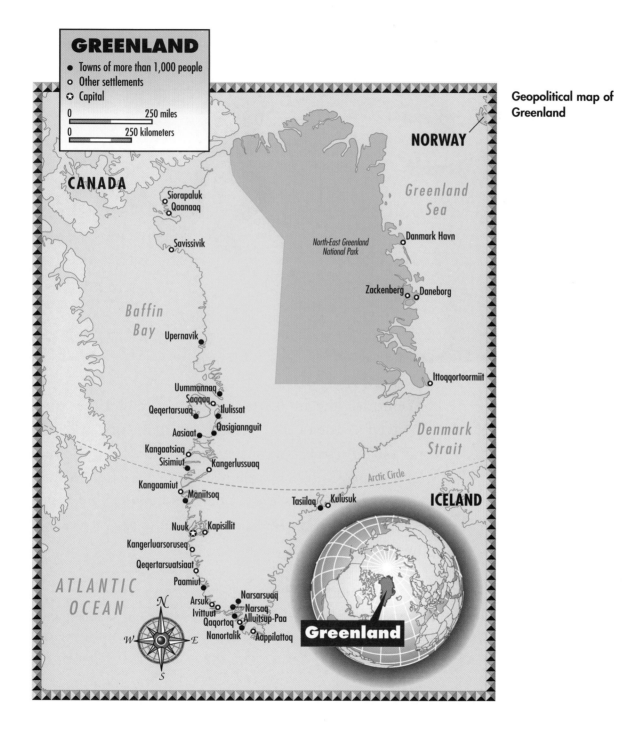

Geopolitical map of
Greenland

GREENLAND

- Towns of more than 1,000 people
- Other settlements
- Capital

0   250 miles

0   250 kilometers

NORWAY

CANADA

*Greenland
Sea*

Siorapaluk
Qaanaaq

Danmark Havn

Savissivik

*North-East Greenland
National Park*

Zackenberg Daneborg

*Baffin
Bay*

Upernavik

Ittoqqortoormiit

Uummannaq
Saqqaq
Qeqertarsuaq Ilulissat
Qasigianguit

*Denmark
Strait*

Aasiaat

Kangaatsiaq
Sisimiut Kangerlussuaq

Arctic Circle

Kangaamiut
Maniitsoq

Tasiilaq Kulusuk

ICELAND

Nuuk Kapisillit

Kangerluarsoruseq

Qeqertarsuatsiaat

*ATLANTIC
OCEAN*

Paamiut

Narsarsuaq

Arsuk Narsaq
Ivittuut Alluitsup-Paa
Qaqortoq
Nanortalik Aappilattoq

Greenland

N
W E
S

Inuit children jump rope in the snow.

For centuries, the Inuit, the native people of Greenland, have survived in one of the harshest environments on Earth. Not only have these people survived, but they have thrived. They have managed to make their lives in the Arctic, where the sun does not shine in winter, where it is impossible to grow crops, and where there is no wood to build houses or to make warming fires.

Ultima Thule

The ancient Greeks referred to a mysterious land— unknown and unknowable—that was so far away it could never be reached. They called it Ultima Thule. Thule itself was thought to be a spot six days' sail to the north. When Knud Rasmussen, an Inuit-Dane who would later become a hero to the Inuit people, established a trading post in the north of Greenland in 1910, he called it Thule.

Not all the people in Greenland are Inuit. Greenland is part of the kingdom of Denmark, a much smaller land hundreds of miles away in Europe. Danes have lived in Greenland for almost three hundred years. About 12 percent of the population is Danish.

The original people of Greenland are part of a larger group of peoples who live throughout the Arctic. They were given the name *Eskimos* long ago. The word may have come from an

This traditionally dressed Inuit girl enjoys the sunshine.

Algonquian Indian word meaning "eater of raw meat." Today, only the Arctic people in Alaska like to be called Eskimos. Everywhere else, *Inuit* is the proper term.

When most Americans or Europeans think of the Inuit, the images that come to mind are actually those of the native people of Greenland. But igloos, whale hunting in kayaks, and polar-bear hunting on the ice are mostly images from the past.

An Inuit hunter and his dog team outside the village of Qaanaaq

Fishing boats in a
Greenland harbor

Today, the Inuit of Greenland are just as likely to be running a tourist business, catching fish to export to other countries, or dancing to pop music.

Any book about the native people of Greenland has to be about two different peoples with different histories. South of the Arctic Circle, the Inuit have lived closely with Europeans since 1721, when settlers arrived from Denmark. But the Inughuit people, who are often called Polar Eskimos, remained isolated in the distant Arctic for another hundred years. Although their lives are changing to become more like the lives of other Greenlanders, the Inughuit still have a culture tied to the sea and the ice.

The lives of all Greenlanders are changing. Their world is no longer so completely isolated. They have things to teach other peoples about living close to nature. And other peoples have both the best and the worst of the distant world to share.

Green and White

THE ISLAND OF GREENLAND COVERS 839,999 SQUARE MILES (2,175,597 sq kilometers), making it the largest island in the world. More than three states of Texas would fit inside Greenland. From north to south, the island is 1,660 miles (2,670 km) long, and it is 652 miles (1,050 km) across. Greenland's coast is deeply jagged. Long fjords, or steep-sided inlets from the sea, cut into the coastline. Because of these fjords, the island's coastline is 24,396 miles (44,087 km) long. That is more than twice as long as the entire coastline of the fifty United States.

Very little of Greenland is habitable. That's because 85 percent of the island is covered by a thick layer of ice called the Inland Ice. This ice sheet is the second-largest on Earth. It covers 668,000 square miles (1,730,000 sq km). Only Antarctica's ice sheet is larger.

Opposite: **The pack ice forms as winter comes.**

A traditional Inuit kayak passes near icebergs on Kangerlussuaq Fjord.

The Arctic landscape is reflected in the Tanqueray Fjord.

Greenland's nearest neighbor is Ellesmere Island, which belongs to Canada. At its nearest point, Ellesmere is only 16 miles (26 km) away from the northwest corner of Greenland. The closest European nation is Iceland. It is 186 miles (299 km) away across the Denmark Strait.

Defining the Arctic

The Arctic is Earth's northern frigid zone, which surrounds the North Pole. Antarctica, the frigid region around the South Pole, is a continent. But much of the Arctic is ocean. In fact, the North Pole is not on land. It is located on sea ice that is floating in the middle of the Arctic Ocean.

Where's the North Pole?

There are actually two North Poles. The geographic North Pole is toward the center of the Arctic Ocean and is where all the lines of longitude meet on a globe. It is at the end of the axis on which Earth rotates.

The second North Pole is the magnetic North Pole. The movement of liquid metal deep inside Earth affects its location, which changes slowly. At the moment, the magnetic North Pole is located on an island west of Ellesmere Island, about 600 miles (1,000 km) south of the geographic North Pole. In the 1950s, the magnetic North Pole was located in Greenland, in an area just north of Qaanaaq.

The northern lights (also called the aurora borealis) are strongest near the magnetic North Pole. This spectacular light display occurs when a flare of charged particles from the sun makes the molecules in the upper atmosphere glow. This happens most easily near the magnetic North Pole.

The Arctic is also sometimes defined as the area north of the tree line. This is the line beyond which trees will not grow. Trees will not grow if the summer months do not average at least 50° Fahrenheit (10° Celsius). Any land north of the tree line is tundra. Tundra is land that remains frozen under the surface all year long. All of Greenland lies north of the tree line.

Cross-country skiers enjoy the Niels Holgersen Nunatakker, an area of glaciers and mountains in East Greeland.

At the equator, the number of hours of daylight in the summer and winter are the same. But as you travel north, there are more hours of daylight in the summer and fewer hours of daylight in the winter. By the time you get to the Arctic Circle, the sun does not set on June 21, the longest day of the year, and it does not rise on December 21, the shortest day of the year.

The Inuit village of Moriussaq during the polar night

Two-thirds of Greenland is located north of the Arctic Circle. This means that most of Greenland is a "land of the midnight sun" in summer and a "land of perpetual darkness" in winter. For several months in the winter, Greenlanders in the north see the stars in the sky at noon.

The Land

There are three parts to Greenland—the ice, the land visible around its edges, and the sea. Greenland is geologically part of North America. Its primary rocks were formed at the same time as the Canadian Shield, the old exposed rock in northern Canada. The rock was formed more than three billion years ago.

Geologists study Greenland's history through its rocks.

Some of the oldest rocks on Earth were found at Isua (also known as Isukasia), about 100 miles (160 km) northeast of Nuuk, Greenland's capital. The rocks are 3.8 billion years old. Those same rocks from Isua have the oldest signs of life on the planet. Carbon traces, probably from algae 3.7 billion years old, were discovered in 1999 by a Greenlandic geologist named Minik Rosing.

Mountain ranges run up both the west and the east coasts. The eastern range is higher than the western range. The highest point in the mountains is Gunnbjørn, at 12,139 feet (3,702 m), which is located near the southeast coast. It is the highest point in the entire Arctic. The lowest point in Greenland is sea level, along the coast. But oddly, most of the land beneath the ice cap is actually lower than sea level because the weight of the ice has pushed it down. If you could remove the ice cap, more of Greenland's landforms would be visible and the sea would flood into many regions.

Finding Out

When Robert Peary and Matthew Henson set out to explore the Arctic in the late 1890s, they thought that Greenland was a continent that extended all the way to the North Pole. Instead, they found that it is an island and that what appears to be land around the North Pole is floating sea ice just a few feet thick.

Kayakers enjoy the magnificent beauty of Kangerlussuaq Fjord

Like Norway, Greenland is famous for its fjords. These are deep inlets with steep sides that cut in from the coastline. One of the longest is Kangerlussuaq, which means "long fjord." The longest fjord in the world is on the opposite side of the island at Ittoqqortoormit. It is 217 miles (350 km) long.

Hundreds of islands lie off the coast of Greenland. The largest island that belongs to Greenland is called Qeqertarsuaq, or Disko Island. It is located on the west side in Disko Bay. The island of Uunartoq has hot springs. People can swim in the hot water and then run through the snow to get dressed.

North Peary Land is a peninsula at the top of the country. Off its coast lies tiny Oodaaq Island. No other piece of land is farther north than this island. Everything farther north is just ice on top of the ocean.

Greenland's Geographic Features

Area: 839,999 square miles (2,175,597 sq km)

Ice sheet: 668,000 square miles (1,730,000 sq km), second-largest on Earth

Distance north to south: 1,660 miles (2,670 km)

Distance east to west: 652 miles (1,050 km)

Coastline: 24,396 miles (44,087 km)

Highest elevation of land: Gunnbjørn, 12,139 feet (3,702 m)

Ice sheet at thickest point: 9,924 feet (3,025 m) thick

Lowest elevation: sea level

Longest fjord: Ittoqqortoormit, longest in the world at 217 miles (350 km)

Land farthest north: Oodaaq Island, the most northerly land on Earth

The Jacobshon Glacier produces more icebergs than any other glacier in the world.

The Ice

The first crossing of Greenland's Inland Ice was led by Norwegian scientist Fridtjof Nansen in 1888. The six-man expedition discovered that Greenland was covered by an unbroken ice cap.

The ice cap is dome-shaped. At its highest point, it is 9,924 feet (3,025 m) thick. The ice cap actually has two high points, or ridges, one in the north and one in the south. The northern ridge is about 950 feet (290 m) higher than the southern one.

The ice cap is not just a single thick sheet of permanent ice. Parts of it are active glaciers. These glaciers are like rivers of ice that continually move outward from the center of the ice cap. On much of Greenland, the glaciers reach all the way to the island's edge. At the edge, pieces of ice break off and tumble into the sea with a thunderous crash. The chunks become icebergs, floating in the sea.

Studying the Ice

Scientists spent seven years drilling on the Greenland ice cap in a program called North GRIP, for North Greenland Ice-core Project. They finally reached bedrock—the rock under the soil—in 2003.

They were not drilling for oil but for knowledge. Their drills brought up 4-inch (10-centimeter) cylinders of ice that were quickly put into freezers to be studied later. Each time the drill brought up another cylinder, called a core, the ice in it came from farther and farther back in time. Researchers would make thin slices of the ice and capture the air in bubbles inside it. By analyzing the air and the ice itself, they could tell what the climate was like in the past.

Study of the Greenland ice cores show that during the last twenty thousand years, the climate has often changed quite abruptly. These climate changes may have played an important role in drastic events that shaped human history.

Sermeq Kujalleq, or Jakobshavn Glacier, flows between mountains and crosses open coastal land before reaching the sea. It has been called the world's fastest-moving glacier. It moves up to 115 feet (35 m) a day. Chunks of Sermeq Kujalleq are constantly breaking off and falling into Disko Bay.

This aerial view of the Greenland ice cap shows how vast the areas of snow and ice are.

The edges of the ice cap are dangerous places. Long, deep cracks called crevasses may be hidden under thin layers of snow. Something as small as a speeding dogsled could break through, sending dogs and people into the deadly crevasse beneath.

The Sea

Besides being covered by ice, Greenland is also surrounded by ice during much of the year. The ice in the sea around Greenland is called

Traveling with the Pack Ice

Norwegian explorer Fridtjof Nansen once watched a piece of driftwood bob in the sea near Greenland. He was intrigued by the way it moved. He became determined to map the currents in the Arctic Ocean.

Nansen had a ship built that was strong enough to withstand being crushed by Arctic pack ice. He found twelve men willing to voyage with him when most people were certain the expedition was doomed. In 1893, they left Norway and headed for the pack ice north of Siberia, in northern Russia. They allowed their ship, the *Fram* (which means "forward") to be frozen into the ice. Nansen and his crew didn't know for sure if the ship would hold up to the pressure.

But it did. After three years of drifting with the pack ice from Siberia, they steered their ship into the Greenland Sea. They had proved that pack ice circles around the North Pole in a clockwise direction.

While the ship was locked in the ice, Nansen and a man named Hjalmar Johansen tried to reach the North Pole. At the time, no one had ever set foot there. They traveled for five months but were still several hundred miles from their goal before being forced to turn back.

pack ice. That means it floats on the surface of the sea and breaks up into chunks in summer. Pack ice is free to move with the currents.

The pack ice contains openings called polynyas. Some are large and permanent, such as the North Water Polynya between Greenland and Ellesmere Island. It is more than 30,000 square miles (77,000 sq km). Polynyas open up in spring and some freeze almost shut in winter. They are found where ocean currents move rapidly over shallow bottoms, preventing the ice from freezing. Traditional Inuit hunters depend on polynyas as places where seals and whales might be found.

Ocean Currents

The ocean currents along Greenland move icebergs around and contribute to the good fishing. The East Greenland Current flows from the Arctic Ocean southward along the east coast of the island. This current carries much pack ice, making the east coast virtually unreachable by ship. Pack ice in this area is often 12 to 15 feet (3.6 to 4.6 m) deep.

Very few people live in east Greenland because it is so cold and inhospitable. The east coast has just two towns, plus a few small settlements.

The East Greenland Current rounds Nunaaq Isua (Cape Farewell)—the southern tip of Greenland. There it meets the warmer Gulf Stream from the south. The turbulence caused by the currents meeting stirs up the food available to fish. Fish of many different kinds are attracted to the area between southern Greenland and Canada's Baffin Island. They, in turn, draw fishing boats from many countries.

The current then continues north as the West Greenland Current. This current is warm enough to make the west coast of the island much more livable. In the west, the coastal water stays fairly free of ice.

The Climate

Greenland's climate ranges from chilly to frigid. On the southern end of the island, the climate is moderated a little by the Gulf Stream. There, the average temperature ranges from 21°F (–6°C) in the winter to 45°F (7°C) in the summer. In the far north, the winter temperature averages –31°F

(–35° C), while the summer averages 39°F (3.6°C). Winter storms in the icy north sometimes have winds up to 100 miles per hour (160 kph).

Greenland gets very little precipitation. In fact, it gets about the same amount as a desert. Any snow that does fall, however, remains on the ground and becomes part of the ice cap. Southern Greenland has more precipitation than the rest of the island. Because it is south of the Arctic Circle, some of that precipitation falls as rain or as snow that melts, providing precious moisture to the green areas.

Global Warming

For thirty years or more, scientists have been warning that Earth is growing warmer. This may be caused by the carbon dioxide spewed into the atmosphere by burning coal and oil. Carbon dioxide and other so-called greenhouse gases hold the sun's heat to the planet's surface.

Scientists are monitoring Greenland's ice cap to see if the ice is melting from global warming. Scientists do not yet know just how global warming will affect the Arctic. Right now, the glaciers around the edge of the island appear to be thinning, while the dome of the ice cap is still growing. Only time and more scientific study will tell what Greenland's future ice cap will look like.

Greenland's "Cities"

The "cities" of Greenland are smaller than most small towns in other parts of the world. All of them are located on water, on the western side of the island, where they can be reached by boat during the winter.

About one-fourth of Greenland's population lives in the capital, Nuuk (below). The second-largest town is Sisimiut. Located north of the Arctic Circle, it is the center of Greenland's fishing industry. Intriguing stone sculptures made by people from all over Greenland are displayed around the town.

Ilulissat (meaning "the icebergs") is the biggest town in northern Greenland. It is located on Disko Bay (right). This bay is one of the great places to see masses of icebergs because Sermeq Kujalleq, one of the fastest-moving glaciers in the world, empties in the bay.

Qaqortoq lies at the southern tip of Greenland at the mouth of the Narsaq fjord. Qaqortoq is home to Hvalsey Church, the largest and best-preserved of the Norse ruins. It is surrounded by wildflower-covered mountains and reindeer and sheep farms. Natural rock formations make up a fascinating collection of sculptures called "Stone and People."

Kangerlussuaq is quite small as Greenland's towns go, but it is the island's most frequently visited town because it is the site of the international airport. The airport was originally built as part of a U.S. air base. One of the few roads in Greenland runs from the airport to the Inland Ice.

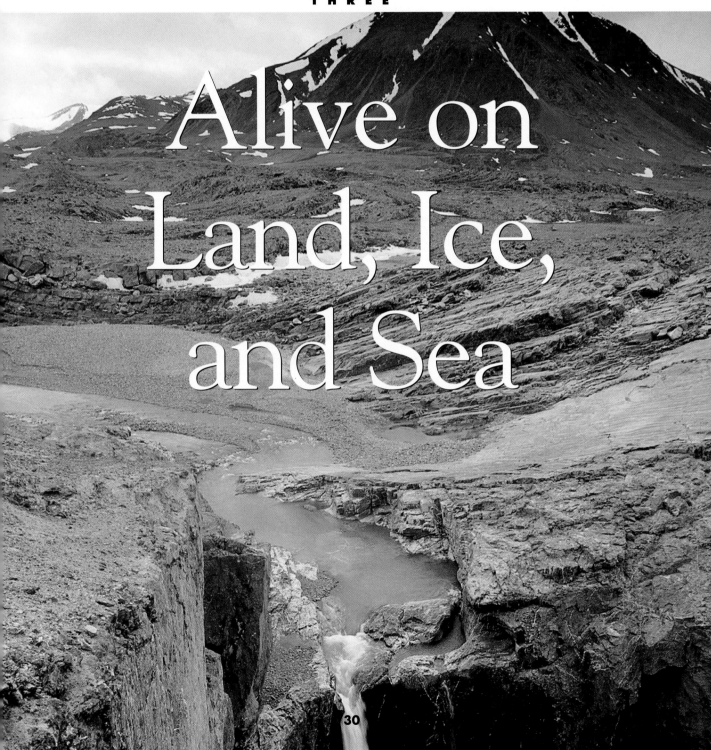

Alive on Land, Ice, and Sea

Halibut is a popular catch.

THE ARCTIC OCEAN CONSISTS OF MORE THAN JUST WATER and ice. It is a rich ecosystem, where many different plants and animals thrive together beneath the ice. Occasional sunlight reaches down into the water through polynyas. In these openings, tiny plants called algae grow. Equally tiny animals feed on the tiny plants. Together, these plants and animals make up the floating food supply called plankton, on which larger animals depend. Fish are drawn to the plankton, and sea mammals are drawn to the fish. As a result, Greenlanders, too, have long depended on the bountiful sea.

Fish

Greenland is surrounded by waters rich with fish. The most important industry in Greenland has long been fishing. Fishing boats go after cod, flounder, and halibut. The Arctic char can be found in both the sea and Greenland's rivers. Trout is another river fish found in Greenland.

Opposite: **Waterfall and Esrum River on Peary Land**

A Greenland shark

Salmon spend much of their lives in the sea, but then they go upriver to spawn. The small settlement of Kapisillit is a fishing village located inland on a fjord about 46 miles (75 km) from Nuuk. *Kapisillit* means "the salmon." The town earned the name because it is the only salmon spawning ground in Greenland.

The only shark found regularly in Arctic waters is the Greenland shark. It is a fairly large animal that is fished for the oil in its liver. Shark oil is used in cosmetics and medicines. The Greenland shark, which is also called the sleeper shark, grows up to 21 feet (6.4 m) long, though most are only half that length. Its flesh is poisonous unless it is boiled and dried. In the past, Inuit used the lower teeth of this shark to cut their hair.

A young ringed seal rests on sea ice.

Mammals at Sea

Several species of seal live around the coasts of Greenland. The most common is the ringed seal. Ringed seals may grow to be 5 feet (1.6 m) long and weigh up to 150 pounds (70 kilograms). They are dark gray with darker spots. The spots often have lighter areas on their edges. These are the seals' "rings." Adult ringed seals usually remain in the ocean at the edge of the ice, but the young stay on the ice itself until they are nearly grown. This leaves them open to attack by hunters who are after the seals' soft fur. Ringed seals stay around Greenland during the winter when other seals travel south.

For many years, harp seal pups were hunted for their beautiful white fur. Fortunately, much of that has now stopped.

The Greenland seal, also called the harp seal, lives throughout the polar region. It is known for the newborn's pure white fur, which lasts only a few weeks. Until recently, baby harp seals were often hunted for their fur, but international efforts have slowed the killing.

Walruses are much bigger than seals. They are so heavy that they cannot support themselves on their fins as most seals can. Instead, they squiggle along on the ground. They are much more graceful in the water, but they often come ashore to lie in the sun. Walruses depend on the water for their food, scraping clams, shrimp, crabs, and other creatures from the seafloor. They sometimes use their tough whiskers to locate the food beneath the mud. Then they blast jets of water from their mouth to uncover it.

Walruses have long been killed for their tusks, which can be carved into tools and other objects. They are considered threatened around Greenland. Some countries have outlawed the importing of walrus tusks.

Walruses are threatened in Greenland because they are hunted for their tusks.

Traditionally, the most important prey for the Inuit in Greenland were whales. Several different kinds of whales spend their summers in Arctic waters. For hundreds of years, whaling ships sailed the seas, hunting whales around the world. Because of this, many whales are now threatened. Most whale hunting is now banned. But the International Whaling Commission has agreed that Greenland's Inuit may kill a certain number of whales because they have always done so to meet their basic needs.

Beluga whales rarely travel to the southern part of Greenland.

The Right Whale

The northern right whale was called the "right" whale by whalers from New England because it was the right one to hunt. It did not swim very fast. It did not sink when it was killed. And it yielded a great deal of blubber for its size. The right whale is about 50 feet (15 m) long. Though the right whale has been protected for more than sixty years, it remains the most endangered of all great whales. Today, probably more than three hundred northern right whales live in the North Atlantic Ocean.

Unicorns

Narwhals are small whales that live around Greenland. Male narwhals produce a single long spiral tusk, which can reach lengths of 7 to 10 feet (2 to 3 m) and weigh as much as 22 pounds (10 kg). The Greenlanders who killed these whales ate its raw skin, called muktaaq. The tusks were sent to Norway, where they were regarded as unicorn horns. Unicorns are mythical horselike creatures with a single horn growing from their forehead. The Norse ground the "unicorn horns" from Greenland into a powder and used it as a medicine.

The bowhead whale has traditionally been one of the most important sources of food, bone, and oil for the northern people. The bowhead can reach 65 feet (20 m) in length. It is fairly slow moving, so it is easier to catch than many other whales. Bowheads live their entire lives in Arctic waters.

Other whales important to the Inuit include the humpback, the fin whale, the killer whale, and the minke. Killer whales feed on the same seals that people catch. Minkes are an important food source for the Polar Inuit. The beluga, or white whale, is small for a whale, only about 18 feet (5.5 m) long. Unlike most whales, the beluga can turn its head. Belugas remain in the Arctic Ocean and rarely come down to the southern end of Greenland.

A breaching killer whale

Mammals on Land

Only a few species of mammals live on the island of Greenland. The smallest are lemmings. These are small rodents similar to hamsters. Most other mammals on

Greenland eat lemmings, as do snowy owls.

Polar bears are big and look like they move slowly. But they can actually move swiftly and with deadly force if challenged. Polar bears can smell food many miles away. Their main prey is the ringed seal. These big white bears are active from March to October. During the rest of the year, the females hibernate in dens built into snow banks while the males continue to roam. Melville Bay, now called Qimusseriarsuaq (meaning "great dogsledding place"), is a nature reserve to protect polar bears. Beluga whales and narwhals also congregate in the bay in the summer.

A mother polar bear with her cub

Musk oxen are closely related to sheep, but they look like shaggy bison. They are large, weighing about 660 pounds (300 kg). Musk oxen get their name from scent glands that are located on the face of the bull. When threatened, the musk ox rubs his face against his legs, which makes the gland emit a strong odor called musk. Musk oxen have two coats of fur. The inner coat is extremely thick and soft. A longer, coarse layer grows through it. These hairs are so long that they may hang down to the ground.

A musk ox family

Caribou are also known as reindeer.

A large wild herd of musk oxen lives around Kangerlussuaq. Most of the year their feeding grounds are covered by a thick layer of ice. They use their heads to butt the ice into pieces so they can reach the plants beneath. This herd is descended from musk oxen introduced from east Greenland in the 1960s. Most other musk oxen live in the national park in northeastern Greenland.

Caribou is the North American name of the deer called reindeer in Europe. They are the only deer in which both males and females have antlers. During the winter, they live on lichen, the tiny mossy plants that grow on rocks. With spring, caribou welcome the tundra plants on which they feed.

Caribou can be found in wild herds wherever there is open land. Greenland is also home to several large reindeer ranches, including one at the southern tip of the island at Isortoq. They are raised mostly for meat and fur. Traditionally, caribou hides were used to make the cargo beds of dogsleds. Antlers were used for runners.

Greenland's National Park

The whole of northeastern Greenland was designated a national park in 1974. Covering almost one-fourth of the island, North-East Greenland National Park is the world's largest national park. It is not meant for sight-seeing. Instead, it is intended to protect the wilderness and the wildlife, especially large mammals, and for weather and ice research. Permits are required to visit the park.

This little ermine blends in with the snow.

The Arctic fox, the Arctic hare, and the ermine (a weasel) all change color with the seasons to protect themselves. When they are on the ice in winter, their fur coats are white. During the summer, when the tundra is a variety of colors, these animals generally turn brown.

Sled Dogs

The Inuit people found their way to Greenland with their sled dogs, which had originated in Asia. For centuries, sleds were the only way to travel on the ice, so dogs were very important to the Inuit. On the west coast north of the Arctic Circle and all along the east coast, the most common animal is the sled dog. The puppies are allowed to run loose until they are almost grown. Then it is time to start training them. They are not pets, but working dogs. Normally, twelve dogs make up a team. They must be trained to work together and depend on each other.

The Greenland sled dog breed has been kept pure. Even today, people are not allowed to bring their own dogs into Greenland in order to keep out diseases not known by Greenland's dogs. Any expedition planning to travel by sled must arrive in Greenland far enough ahead of time to get and train their dog teams.

Nesting Birds

Many birds nest along the coast of Greenland in spring and summer. Thousands gather on open flat ground and in small niches on steep cliffs. The thick-billed murre, guillemot, eider ducks, and other sea ducks are among the visitors. Eiders are among the largest ducks in the Northern Hemisphere. Native people often catch them and make soft blankets from their skins.

The Greenland white-fronted goose and the pink-footed goose spend summers in Greenland. Western Greenland attracts peregrine falcons and gyrfalcons. Snowy owls live on

The white-fronted goose lives in Greenland during the summer.

The Original Penguin

Traditionally, one of the most important birds for the Inuit was the great auk, a penguinlike bird related to the puffin. When explorers first saw the birds in 1588, they gave it the name *penguin*, meaning "white head." Later, when the birds now called penguins were seen in the Southern Hemisphere, the name was transferred to them.

The great auk was a diving bird that nested along the southern Greenland coast. They were large birds, about 25 inches (64 cm) tall, so they provided a lot of meat and fat for the Inuit diet. Because they were flightless, they were easy prey to hunters. Auks became extinct in 1844.

the northern tundra but head farther south during the worst of winter. The ptarmigan is a brown game bird that is widely hunted in the tundra.

The number of birds that nest in Greenland used to be much larger. Some nesting spots that once welcomed hundreds of thousands of birds are not even used anymore. The government has outlawed hunting for some species in spring and summer so that they can breed safely.

The National Flower

The national flower of Greenland is the French willow, or large-flowered rosebay. The Inuit call it *niviarsiaq*, which means "young woman." It is pink with purple veins and grows on the slopes of the mountains.

Plant Life

Most of Greenland is covered by ice. But even in those few places where the ground is exposed, the soil beneath the surface stays frozen even in summer. This is called permafrost. The few feet of soil above the permafrost is swampy. The water cannot sink into the ground because it is blocked by the frozen soil.

This swampy soil, called tundra, supports some wildflower shrubs. Even a few small trees manage to survive in places where they are protected from the dry, cold winds. In the far north, where the climate is very dry, there are usually no plants, just rock.

Many plants in Greenland have fine hairs on their stems and leaves. These hairs

Bluebells flourish in the summer sunshine.

trap the warmth of sunlight. Pretty flowers often grow in dark spots among rocks because the darkness absorbs the heat from the sunlight, keeping the plants warm so they can flourish.

More than 250 species of plants can be seen during the summer. These include yellow arctic poppies, cotton grass, and pink campions. Cloudberries, bilberries, and cranberries grow on low bushes. During the short summer season, the wildflowers burst into bloom and the berry bushes are laden with fruit. Then in the fall, the tundra turns vivid autumn colors.

The entire island of Greenland is north of the tree line. Some birch trees, however, grow in sheltered valleys of the south, where they can reach 20 feet (6 m) high. Beyond the sheltered areas, dwarf birch and willow are common, but they are so low-growing that they look more like a ground cover plant than a tree.

This Arctic birch looks more like ground cover than a tree.

C H A P T E R

F O U R

Greenland's Story

PEOPLE FIRST ARRIVED IN GREENLAND MORE THAN 4,000 years ago. They came to Greenland from the west and settled at the northeastern corner of the island. Evidence of their dwellings has been found there. They are called the Independence I people, because they lived near Independence Bay. They were Stone Age people who made tiny blades and arrowheads out of rock. Archaeologists have found bone needles, showing that the people also sewed clothing and tents.

It is likely that the Independence I people invented the igloo. They also used kayaks. The climate was warmer at the time than it is today, and they were able to fish in the fjords of the north.

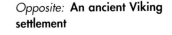

Opposite: **An ancient Viking settlement**

Kayaks on the beach

Another group of people arrived in western and southern Greenland after the Independence I people arrived. They are known as the Saqqaq people. They lived around Disko Bay, Sisimiut, and Nuuk. The Saqqaq probably moved with the hunting season. They, too, made small tools, but they had much more driftwood available to work with than the people in the north did.

By about 600 B.C., a possibly different group of people called Independence II were living in the northeast. The Independence II people lived in good-sized communities. Scientists found one site that had more than 400 dwellings.

An iceberg in Disko Bay

This may have been a place where many different extended families would get together on special occasions. Normally, the families would likely have traveled in much smaller groups.

Another group, called the Dorset culture, lived in the south by about 500 B.C. The Dorset people hunted sea mammals with spears in open boats called umiaks. They began to trade with neighboring peoples. The Dorset people left many small animal and human figures carved from ivory, bones, and antlers.

The Inuit's Ancestors

The last group of native people to arrive in Greenland is called the Thule culture. Traveling east from Alaska in pursuit of bowhead whales in around A.D. 900, they overran the Dorset people. The Thule people are named for the area where scientists first located their artifacts.

An Inuit mask

The Thule hunted land animals, especially musk oxen and caribou. They also learned to travel by dogsled. The Thule people brought kayaks to Greenland, along with bows and arrows. They are the ancestors of all the Inuit found across Canada and Greenland today.

Vikings Arrive in Greenland

The Vikings were seagoing people from Norway, in northern Europe. They were the first Europeans to see Greenland. In about A.D. 930, a Viking named Gunnbjørn Ulfsson was blown off course and discovered the island. Today, the island's highest peak bears his name.

Erik the Red battles an Icelandic chief.

The existence of the island was little more than a tale until 982. That year, a Viking named Erik Thorvaldsson, who was known as Erik the Red, was forced to leave Iceland because he had killed someone. His wife and children probably went with him, along with other men and women.

Erik sailed to Greenland, where he spent three years exploring. By then, he thought it would be safe to return to Iceland. When he was not welcomed home, he decided to return to the island and settle down. He called his destination Greenland in the hope that the name would attract other settlers. It worked. In the summer of 986, ships carrying 350 people and their livestock landed in Greenland.

They established two colonies, both on the west coast of the island. There were no natives there, although long-abandoned dwellings gave the new settlers a start. It was many months before Greenland's new settlers met an Inuit.

Later, the Vikings in Iceland passed on their history in tales called sagas. *The Greenlanders' Saga* was written down in about 1300. *The Saga of Eirik the Red* was written soon after.

Vikings in Canada

A man named Bjarni Herjulfsson had been away from Iceland when the colonists left for Greenland. Herjulfsson set out to find them but lost his way. Instead, he explored southward down the coast of North America. He probably never landed in Greenland.

In 1001, Erik's son, Leif Eriksson, led an expedition southward from Greenland in search of trees, which were needed to build houses and boats. The expedition spent the winter in Newfoundland, in what is now Canada, and called their temporary home Vinland.

Erik's other son, Thorvald, soon followed in his brother's footsteps. In 1004, on the Labrador Peninsula of Canada, he and his party may have been the first Europeans to make contact with Native Americans. The meeting did not go well, and Thorvald was killed.

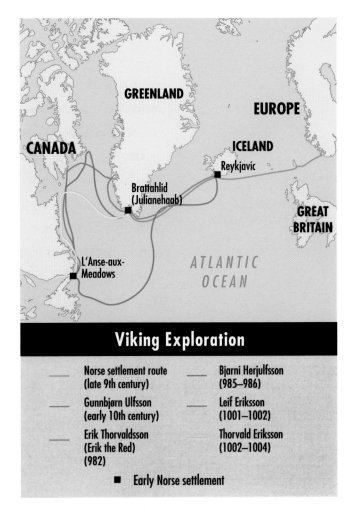

GREENLAND

EUROPE

CANADA

ICELAND

Reykjavic

Brattahlid
(Julianehaab)

GREAT
BRITAIN

L'Anse-aux-
Meadows

ATLANTIC
OCEAN

Viking Exploration

Norse settlement route (late 9th century)	Bjarni Herjulfsson (985–986)
Gunnbjørn Ulfsson (early 10th century)	Leif Eriksson (1001–1002)
Erik Thorvaldsson (Erik the Red) (982)	Thorvald Eriksson (1002–1004)
■ Early Norse settlement	

During coming years, European Greenlanders often traveled to Labrador for trees. They continued to make the trip until they abandoned Greenland itself.

The Norse Life

At its peak, the Norse colony in Greenland may have had as many as five thousand people. They were located on about three hundred farms in two areas called the Eastern Settlement and the Western Settlement. Both were on the southwestern coast of the island. The Eastern Settlement was at the site of present-day Narsaq, at the tip of the island. The Western Settlement was near Nuuk. Erik the Red built a farm called Brattahlid in the Western Settlement. Ruins of his farm are still visible. Some Inuit lived near the settlements, but they seemed to have left the settlers alone.

The ruins of the walls the Vikings built are still visible today.

The Norse Greenlanders hunted, fished, and raised cattle and sheep. They also traded walrus and caribou skins, polar bear and seal fur, and sheep's wool to Norwegians for European goods.

Traditionally, Norse people had believed in many gods. But around the time they settled Greenland, many were converting to Christianity. Several churches were built in each settlement. The colonists developed a parliament, or lawmaking body. In 1261, the settlers of Greenland followed the lead of the Norse in Iceland and accepted rule by the Norwegian king. They thought this would improve trade. Better trade never happened, but bigger changes were about to come.

The End of Settlement

During the time of Norse settlement of Greenland, the area was relatively warm. But around 1300, the region entered a period that has been called the Little Ice Age. Temperatures dropped so much that the people in Greenland could no longer grow crops. Their livestock froze. The pack ice was so thick that ships could not make it to harbor.

The Western Settlement was abandoned by 1350. In the fifteenth century, the Eastern Settlement also disappeared. Nobody is sure what happened to them. Some say that it simply got too cold, even for Vikings. Others say that the Inuit from the north attacked them, or that the last of the Norse married into the Inuit culture. It has even been suggested that a new type of caterpillar arrived in Greenland and ate all the plants that livestock usually graze on. Archaeological evidence shows that the Norse continued living in Greenland until 1480 or so.

The Last Word

In 1408, a wedding was held at Hvalsey Church. The priest who performed the ceremony sent a description of the wedding back to Iceland. This is the last mention in writing of the Norse people living in Greenland. Today, visitors can tour the ruins of the Hvalsey Church.

And Still They Came

The Inuit were not alone for long after the Norse left Greenland. Starting in the 1500s, ships from Europe began to appear in the area. They were hunting for whales. They used the whale blubber to make oil for lamps. Men from the whaling ships often traded goods with the native people.

Some ships from Europe were also hunting for the legendary Northwest Passage, a route that would take ships quickly from the Atlantic to the Pacific. Without this route, ships had to spend many months rounding South America.

English sea captain Martin Frobisher "rediscovered" Greenland in 1576 when he was trying to find the Northwest Passage. He and the sailors aboard his ship *Gabriel* saw Greenland, but they were unable to get through the pack ice to reach it.

Portrait of the navigator Martin Frobisher

The Norwegian government had not totally given up on finding the Norse colonists. Between 1607 and 1654, it sent six ships to trade and to hunt for descendants from the early settlements. They found no one, and they did not stay.

"We Are Alone"

In the meantime, far to the north, the people called Polar Eskimos, or Inughuit, were living their lives in isolation. They had almost no communication with the Inuit in the south. They had lost the use of bows and arrows and so did not eat caribou meat. They had also lost the use of the kayak and so could hunt only those animals that came up onto the ice.

When Captain John Ross found the Polar Eskimos in 1818, they said to him, "We are alone in the world." There's no telling whether they actually thought this was true or if the translator made a mistake.

John Ross encounters Polar Eskimos in 1818 near Cape York.

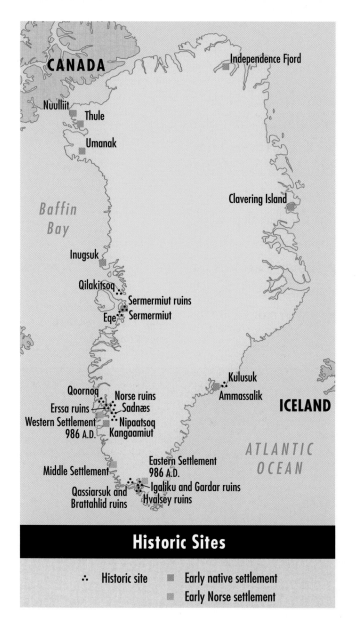

CANADA

Independence Fjord

Nuulliit
Thule
Umanak

Baffin
Bay

Clavering Island

Inugsuk

Qilakitsoq
Sermermiut ruins
Eqe
Sermermiut

Kulusuk
Ammassalik

ICELAND

Qoornoq
Norse ruins
Erssa ruins
Sadnæs
Western Settlement
986 A.D.
Nipaatsoq
Kangaamiut

ATLANTIC
OCEAN

Eastern Settlement
986 A.D.

Middle Settlement

Qassiarsuk and
Brattahlid ruins
Igaliku and Gardar ruins
Hvalsey ruins

Historic Sites

∴ Historic site   ■ Early native settlement

■ Early Norse settlement

They did not remain alone for long. In the 1850s, a final Inuit migration took place from Baffin Island north through Ellesmere and then to northern Greenland. Led by a shaman named Qillaq, a group of perhaps sixty people reached the northern shores of Greenland. They reintroduced both kayaks and bows and arrows to the Inughuit living there.

Most of the Inughuit have remained fairly isolated, even though they are the people who helped explorers conquer the Arctic Ocean and the North Pole. Today, when many Greenlanders are hoping to rediscover their hunting past, it is the Inughuit who can come closest to teaching them the old ways.

New Settlement

In 1721, Europeans once again came to Greenland, this time to stay. The missionary Hans Egede thought there were probably still descendants of the Norse settlers living among the native people. He thought it was important that they be converted to Christianity. He convinced the Danish, who had claimed Greenland, to let him set up a mission and trading post.

Egede and forty-five followers arrived on the island. He was disappointed to find no sign of the Norse settlers among the Inuit. Instead, he began converting the Inuit.

Egede and his followers founded a settlement called Godthaab, which is now Nuuk. They also began trading with Denmark. This was the beginning of Greenland's life as an active colony of Denmark.

A report Egede sent back to Norway describing Greenland was published. His stories fascinated people, and the book was translated into several languages. Danish settlers began to move to Greenland. The earliest immigrants weren't always there by choice; many of them were convicts from Denmark's prisons.

Going "a Whale Catching"

In his book on Greenland, missionary Hans Egede (1686–1758) describes whaling by the Inuit: "When they go a Whale catching, they put on their best Gear or Apparel, as if they were going to a Wedding-Feast, fancying that if they did not come cleanly and neatly dressed, the Whale, who can't bear sloven and dirty Habits, would shun them and fly from them."

A Norwegian named Jakob Severin supported Egede in his trading work. Severin gained the right to carry out all trade with Greenland. He prevented other ships from landing in Greenland to trade. His ships even carried out a gun battle with the Dutch, who wanted to be able to trade. Severin's name was given to the town of Jakobshavn, which is now called Ilulissat.

In 1776, the Danish government took control of trade with Greenland. It set up the Royal Greenlandic Trading Company, which, in many ways, ran Greenland and its economy for the next century and a half. Greenland was closed to foreigners from 1782 to 1950.

Little was done to improve the standard of living. Most Danes who moved to Greenland worked for the government, but many grew to like the country. They stayed and raised their families, sometimes marrying into Inuit families.

Outsiders heard about Greenland mostly in terms of the explorers who went there to use its northern end as a stepping-stone to the North Pole. These explorers brought the outside world—with both its benefits and its problems—to the Inughuit.

In the 1920s, Norway became one of the major whaling countries along the Greenland coast. It claimed that it had historical rights to part of the east coast. Denmark moved some Inuit to new villages along the east coast, hoping that would stop Norway from claiming part of the island.

The Danes took the quarrel with Norway to the Court of International Justice. In 1933, the court decided that the whole of Greenland belonged to Denmark.

The First to the Pole

American explorer Robert Edwin Peary (1856–1920) was determined to be the first person to reach the North Pole. He made eight expeditions in twenty-three years trying. He traveled through Greenland on each of these trips, working with and living with the Inughuit.

A native of Pennsylvania, Peary was in the U.S. Navy when he made his first trip to Greenland in 1886, exploring the ice cap. In the navy, he met Matthew Henson, an African American from Virginia, who was also caught up in the dream of finding the pole. Together, they lived among the Inughuit in northern Greenland to learn their survival skills. Inuit legend calls Henson *Mahri-Pahluk*, meaning "Matthew the kind one."

Between 1893 and 1909, Peary, Henson, and a number of different Inughuit made several expeditions toward the North Pole. Each journey took Peary closer. On one journey, he froze his toes and had to have eight of them amputated.

Finally, in 1908, Peary allowed his ship to be frozen into the pack ice. He waited through the four months of winter night, preparing his equipment. On March 1, 1909, he, Henson, and twenty-two other men set out across the ice. On April 6, Peary planted an American flag in the ice. Peary became a hero to the American people.

But was it actually the North Pole? Peary went down in record books as having been the first to reach the pole. But from the day he arrived back in New York, people questioned whether he had succeeded. Another explorer named Frederick Cook claimed to have reached the North Pole first. Peary had no way to

prove his progress and his success. He insisted that the world just take his word for it. The Inuit themselves had no doubt that Peary had reached the pole.

A study by the First International Congress on the North Pole in 1983 decided that there was not enough data to reach a conclusion. They added that the first person who had evidence that he had reached the North Pole was American Ralph Plaisted. He arrived at the pole in April 1968—by snowmobile.

The Man Who Knew the Inuit

Knud Rasmussen (1879–1933), a Greenlander of both Inuit and Danish descent, introduced the world to the Inuit. He was born at Ilulissat and grew up in both Greenland and Denmark. The news of Robert Peary reaching the North Pole in 1909 prompted Rasmussen to return to Greenland from Denmark.

Knud Rasmussen was of both Inuit and Danish descent.

Working with explorer Peter Freuchen, he established a trading post, a clinic, and a communications center on North Star Bay. He called it Thule; the Inughuit called it Qaanaaq.

Rasmussen and Freuchen made several journeys through the Arctic. The most important lasted three and a half years. They traveled across the polar north, tracing in reverse the original Inuit journey from Siberia to Greenland. During this journey, Rasmussen talked to the Inuit people. He studied their ways of life, heard their stories, ate their food, and helped them hunt. From them, he learned the history of the ancient peoples who inhabited the polar regions. Most of what is known today stems from Rasmussen's notes.

Rasmussen always respected the Inuit, and he became a hero to them. When he died of food poisoning in 1933, the northernmost part of Greenland was named for him.

World War II

Tensions in Europe were rising throughout the 1930s. Germany was acting aggressively toward its neighbors, and in 1939 World War II began. Two years later, the United States would join the fight against the Germans.

Germany had invaded Denmark in 1940 and quickly took control of it. All communication with Greenland stopped. The government in Greenland decided that since communication was broken, it had the right to run its country in its own fashion. And that fashion included fighting the Germans.

Germany secretly put men ashore on the northeast coast of Greenland to man a weather station. The men radioed weather information back to the war zones and the German air force. Several times, members of the Greenland Sled Patrol came across German weather stations. Several Greenlanders were killed, and others were briefly taken captive. For the most part, however, it was Germans who were captured and turned over to the Americans.

The Lost Squadron

During World War II, a squadron consisting of six P-38 Lightning fighters and two B-17 bombers made emergency landings on Greenland's ice cap. The people were rescued, but the aircraft were abandoned on the ice. Over the next fifty years, ice built up over them.

In 1992, a Kentucky businessman paid for the recovery of one of the airplanes, a Lightning. At that time, it was 268 feet (83 m) below the surface of the ice. Holes were chopped in the ice so that the plane could be brought up piece by piece. Over the next ten years, the aircraft was restored in complete detail. On October 26, 2002, the sixty-year-old airplane, now called *Glacier Girl*, flew over Kentucky.

Americans were in Greenland because the southern part of the island had become vital to the war. Great Britain desperately needed American planes. German submarines ruled the North Atlantic. Any ship carrying planes to Europe would be attacked. So the American airplanes had to be flown from the United States. An American military airbase, called Bluie West 1, was established at Narsarsuaq on the southern coast of Greenland. Thousands of military planes stopped there to refuel on their way to war.

Americans in Greenland

After the war, the United States decided that it needed an air base in the north. It tried to buy Greenland from Denmark. The Danes refused. But as thanks for the wartime help, they gave the United States the right to build an air base on the west coast of Greenland at Thule. In 1951, 12,000 American soldiers arrived at the new secret military base at Thule.

The Inuit were pretty much left alone for two years. Then in 1953, the Americans wanted to expand their base. They forced about twenty-seven Inuit families to move to a new village farther north. The new Thule is 62 miles (100 km) north of the old one. That short distance took the native people away from their traditional walrus-hunting grounds. The new Thule, which is now called Qaanaaq, is located only 870 miles (1,400 km) from the North Pole. It is the world's northernmost town, though there is a small settlement farther north.

In 1968, an American B-52 bomber carrying four nuclear weapons crashed onto the sea ice near Thule. The aircraft burned. The United States agreed to clean up all traces of the accident, including dangerous radioactive materials from the bombs. The U.S. military claimed to have done so. Many years later, though, it became clear that one of the bombs had not been found and was still lying in the sea off Greenland's coast. High levels of radiation are recorded in the area. Many Greenlanders remain bitter about this and other pollution caused by the military. They are also still angry about having to relocate Thule.

Home Rule—Self Government

For much of history, Greenlanders did not have full rights as Danish citizens. Then in 1953, the Danish constitution was changed to make Greenland a full part of Denmark, rather than just a colony. That meant that Greenlanders now had the same rights as any Danes.

Becoming full citizens got many Greenlanders thinking about independence. In 1978, the idea of independence for Greenland was put to a vote in both Greenland and Denmark. It was approved, and Greenland became a mostly independent nation. Denmark kept control of Greenland's international affairs and defense. But Greenland's new Home Rule Government controlled everything else.

Most people in Greenland are still not satisfied, though. An estimated 80 percent of Greenlanders want to be completely independent of Denmark and want the U.S. military off the island. They want nothing less than full control of their island.

Matters of
Government

For hundreds of years, Greenland was controlled by Denmark, a European nation far from the cold waters around Greenland. For much of that time, Greenlanders had little say in how their country was run. The first government in which the native people took part was a Board of Guardians, which formed in 1857. Danes and men with known seal-hunting skills were allowed on the board. In 1908, when local municipal councils were formed, only native Greenlanders were allowed on them.

In 1953, Denmark changed its constitution. Greenlanders were now full citizens of Denmark. Any laws passed in

Opposite: **A typical wooden building erected by the Danish government**

Greenland's Flag

Greenland's flag was designed by an artist named Thue Christiansen. It was adopted by the Home Rule Government on June 21, 1985. It uses the same colors as the Danish flag. Christiansen himself describes the flag this way: "The large white part in the flag symbolizes the ice cap, and our fjords are represented by the red part in the circle. The white part of the circle symbolizes the icebergs and the pack ice, and the large red part in the flag represents the ocean."

Parliamentary chambers at
Christianborg Palace

Denmark also applied in Greenland unless the laws stated otherwise. The voters in Greenland elected two members of the Danish parliament.

In 1979, voters in both Greenland and Denmark agreed that Greenland should have an independent government. Greenlanders got their own parliament, their own prime minister, and their own say in most matters of government. Denmark still controls Greenland's national defense and some of its international trade, but Greenlanders themselves now make most decisions.

The time since Greenland's Home Rule Government was formed has been hectic. It has been described as a passage through adolescence into adulthood. As Greenlanders gained many more rights, some of them began to think that they should be completely independent of Danish rule. In 2005, the leading political party was Siumut, meaning "forward party." This party wants greater independence from Denmark. Another party, the Inuit Party, is in favor of breaking away from Denmark entirely.

Greenland is a parliamentary democracy within a constitutional monarchy. The chief of state of Greenland is the king or queen of Denmark. The king or queen has only those powers granted by the Danish constitution. Since 1972, the chief of state has been Queen Margrethe II. She is represented in Greenland by a high commissioner, whom she appoints. The high commissioner is mostly involved in overseeing elections, problems of family law, and any matters that affect Denmark.

Queen Margrethe II of Denmark

The head of government is the prime minister, who is elected by the Greenlandic Parliament. The prime minister's official residence is the home built in 1728 by Godthaab founder Hans Egede.

The prime minister and a board of between two and six members form the *Landsstyre*, the Home Rule Government. The members of the Landsstyre are appointed by the parliament.

The parliament, or *Landsting*, has only one house. The thirty-one members of parliament are elected every four years. All citizens over the age of eighteen can vote.

The Judicial System

Greenland's judicial system consists of several district courts. Most cases are tried in these courts. Major cases or appeals are tried by the Greenland High Court, or *Landsret*. The decisions made by this court can be appealed to the Supreme Court in Denmark. There are no prisons in Greenland. If someone commits a very serious crime, such as murder, he or she may be sent to Denmark to prison.

Local Government

The country is broken into three large districts, called *landsdele*. Within each district are eighteen municipalities, or towns. A mayor and a district council run each of the eighteen municipalities. They are elected every four years.

The town of Jakobshavn

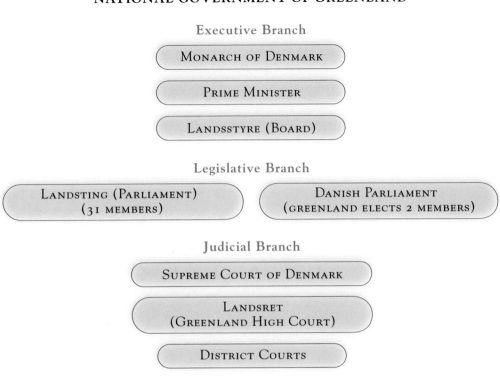

NATIONAL GOVERNMENT OF GREENLAND

Executive Branch

Monarch of Denmark

Prime Minister

Landsstyre (Board)

Legislative Branch

Landsting (Parliament)
(31 members)

Danish Parliament
(Greenland elects 2 members)

Judicial Branch

Supreme Court of Denmark

Landsret
(Greenland High Court)

District Courts

Government Control of the Economy

For more than two hundred years, Greenlanders have depended on the Royal Greenlandic Trading Company. This is the arm of the Danish government that has built Greenland's buildings, roads, power lines, and airports. It has also kept Greenlanders supplied with everything they needed. Greenlanders have not been allowed to trade with any other country or company.

Greenland's Home Rule Government took over the trading company in 1986. It soon split the company up. One part is responsible for trade in the ten towns that are open to the sea all year. The second takes care of trade in the outlying areas and in towns that are more isolated. The second company also has charge of the postal service for the whole island.

The Home Rule Government also owns Royal Arctic Line, a shipping company that has the main contract to carry passengers and goods between Greenland and Denmark. It is run jointly with a Danish shipping company.

These companies do not need to be self-supporting. The government gives them support because Greenland could not function if only privately owned businesses ran trade for the whole country. Government control ensures that goods sent to outlying areas are no more expensive than those in the main settlements. If private companies were doing the trading, they would charge more for goods sent to remote settlements because of the cost of shipping them there.

Going Polar

The Inuit Circumpolar Conference (ICC) was established in 1977. It represents the approximately 150,000 people living in Arctic regions around the world. The Inuit are found in the United States, Canada, Greenland, and Russia. The organization's General Assembly meets every four years. The organization's main goals are to protect the ecological health of the entire Arctic region and to make certain that the Inuit play a role in any decisions affecting the development of the Arctic. The ICC has developed the University of the Arctic, which links up institutions of higher learning in all the related countries.

The National Anthem

The words to Greenland's national anthem, "Nunarput Utpqqarsiammgpravot" (You Our Ancient Land), were written by Danish priest and poet Henrik Lund (1875–1948). His poem, which was written in 1912, became the national anthem in 1916. There is a Henrik Lund Museum at Narsaq. A second national anthem called "Land of Great Length" has been recognized since 1979.

Greenlandic Lyrics

Nunarput, utoqqarsuanngoravit niaqqut ulissimavoqq qiinik.
Qitornatit kissumiaannarpatit tunillugit sineriavit piinik.

Akullequtaastut merletutut ilinni perotugut tamaani
kalaallinik imminik taajumavugut niaqquit ataqqinartup saani.

Atortillugillu tamaasa pisit ingerlaniarusuleqaagut,
nutarterlugillu noqitsigisatit siumut, siumut piumaqaagut.

Inersimalersut ingerlanerat tungaalitsiterusuleqaarput,
oqaatsit "aviisit" qanoq kingunerat atussasoq erinigileqaarput.

Taqilluni naami atunngiveqaaq, kalaallit siumut makigitsi.
Inuttut inuuneq pigiuminaqaaq, saperasi isumaqaleritsi.

English Lyrics

Our country, who's become so old your head all covered with white hair.
Always held us, your children, in your bosom providing the riches of your coasts.

As middle children in the family we blossomed here Greenland,
we want to call ourselves before your proud and honorable head.

With a burning desire to develop what you have to give, renewing,
Removing your obstacles our desire to move is forward, forward.

The way of matured societies is our zealous goal to attain;
the effect of speech and letters we long to behold.

Humbleness is not the course Greenland wake up and be proud!
A dignified life is our goal; couragously [sic] take a stand.

Nuuk: Did You Know?

The capital of Greenland is Nuuk (below), meaning "promontory," or a high point of land. Nuuk is located on the southwest coast on Nuuk Fjord. It is almost completely surrounded by water. Because of the fairly warm current that moves around the southern tip of the island, Nuuk's harbor remains open all year.

Nuuk is the largest town in Greenland, with a population of 13,889. About one-fourth of all Greenlanders live in Nuuk or in two nearby towns that might be called suburbs. Although the area around Nuuk was first inhabited perhaps four thousand years ago, it was officially founded in 1728 by Hans Egede.

Wooden combs
discovered near
a Viking settlement

Mount Sermitsiaq looms over Nuuk. During warmer weather, its jagged landscape features beautiful waterfalls. *Sermitsiaq* is also the name of Greenland's newspaper, which is published in Nuuk.

The Katuaq Cultural Center is a stunning building, with walls that curve in waves like the sea or windblown snow. The center, which opened in 1997, was founded as a central site for preserving and demonstrating Greenlandic culture—literature, dance, music, art, and historical artifacts (above). Greenland National Museum and Archives is in charge of preserving the Greenlandic culture and official papers. Some of the exhibits display items that were returned to Greenland from museums in Denmark.

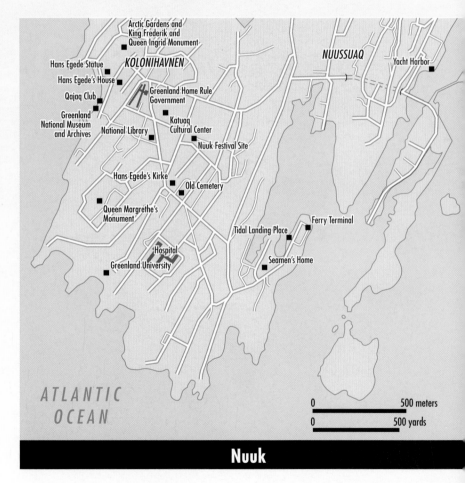

Nuuk

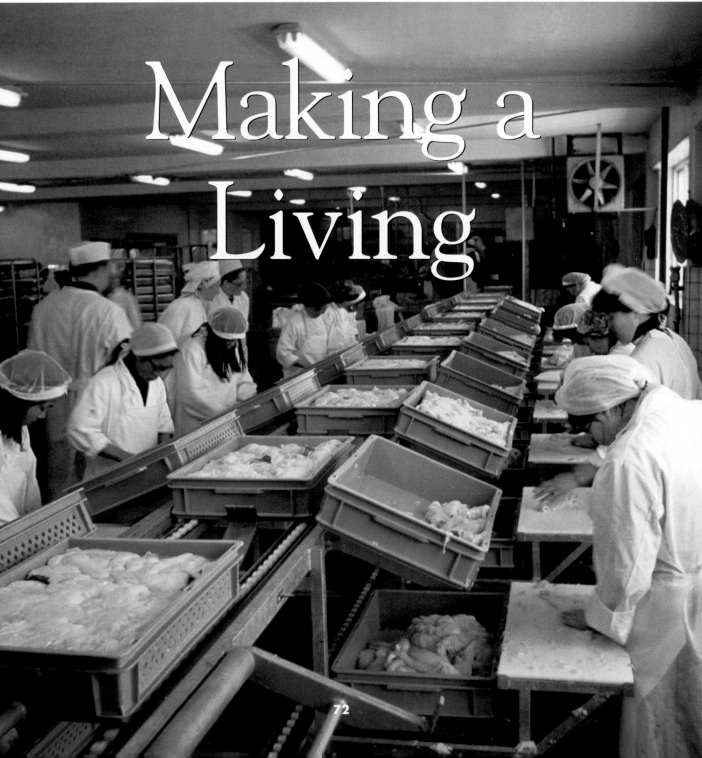

CHAPTER SIX

Making a Living

GREENLAND'S ECONOMY IS DEPENDENT UPON DENMARK. About 60 percent of all exports from Greenland go to Denmark, while Denmark (82.6%), Norway, and Sweden provide the imports that Greenlanders need to survive.

The Home Rule Government is the largest employer in Greenland. More than eight thousand Greenlanders do such things as supervise and maintain apartment buildings, work in construction, teach, and serve as communications experts.

Opposite: **Workers at a fish factory**

Apartments in Greenland's capital

Another five thousand Greenlanders work in fishing. But several thousand others have little to do. Unemployment in recent years has been close to 10 percent. Greenlanders are not satisfied with this situation. Step by step, they are doing what they can to change the economic facts of life on their large island.

Fishing and Sealing

Greenland's first fish-processing plant was established in Sisimiut in 1927. The harbor there attracted shrimp-fishing vessels, and Sisimiut became the island's second-largest town. Several thousand Greenlanders now work in the country's fishing industry, which is controlled by Royal Greenland.

Money in Greenland

Greenland uses the Danish krone ("crown") as its money. The plural is kroner, and the abbreviation is DKr. The smaller unit is the øre. There are 100 øre to a krone. Greenland has just one bank. It is located in Nuuk.

Almost all of Greenland's exports consist of fish, other sea- food, and fish products.

The main catch is shrimp. More than 70,000 tons are processed every year for the world market. Cod was once the most important fish in Greenland. But it has become scarce. Halibut is now more important to Greenland's fishing industry.

Seal skins are stretched on ropes to dry.

Nearly one-fifth of Greenlanders are involved in hunting. The Inughuit in the north have always depended on being able to trade sealskins and furs as well as walrus ivory for goods they needed. The Greenlanders needed the skins to make kayaks and to line their homes. Those uses have virtually disappeared, and many nations now frown on the sale of skins and tusks. This has driven many Inughuit into poverty.

It is estimated that Greenlanders still kill about eighty thousand ringed seals every year. The meat is sold locally, but the skins are sold to the Great Greenland Tannery at Qaqortoq.

Minerals

The oldest industry on Greenland is the mining of cryolite, which is also called Greenland spar. Cryolite, used in processing aluminum, is rare. It is found only in three or four places in the world. In Greenland, there is a major cryolite mine at Ivittuut and a smaller one at Arsuk.

Oil has been found on the west coast and near Jameson Land in east Greenland. Valuable deposits of diamonds, gold, niobium, tantalite, uranium, and iron have also been found, but few of them have been mined yet. Some coal, marble, zinc, lead, and silver have been mined.

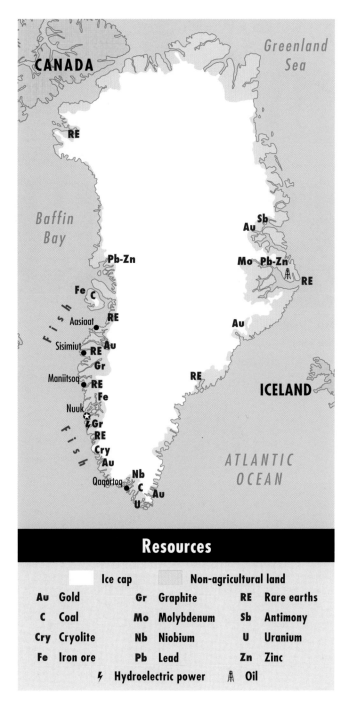

Resources

	Ice cap	Non-agricultural land	
Au	Gold	Gr Graphite	RE Rare earths
C	Coal	Mo Molybdenum	Sb Antimony
Cry	Cryolite	Nb Niobium	U Uranium
Fe	Iron ore	Pb Lead	Zn Zinc
⚡ Hydroelectric power		⚒ Oil	

Fish are dried for use later in the year.

What Greenland Grows, Makes, and Mines

Agriculture

Greenland has no arable land; vegetables are grown in both gardens and greenhouses.

Sheep and domesticated reindeer are grown on available pastureland in the south.

Manufacturing

90 percent of exports are fish products, especially shrimp and Greenland halibut.

Mining

Mines are few, primarily zinc and lead; gold may become important in the future.

Agriculture

Greenland is too cold for most farming. The growing season is too short for crops to mature and be harvested. In the south, land is used for sheep farming. The sheep farmers grow grasses that can feed the sheep during the long winter. The farmers take pride in knowing they and their sheep do not depend on imported food. There are several caribou, or reindeer, farms in Greenland. The animals are raised as a source of meat.

Reindeer are raised for their meat.

A New Kind of Power

Until recently, 100 percent of Greenland's power needs were met by imported oil. Then, in 1993, Greenland's first hydroelectric power plant was built south of Nuuk. The plant supplies Nuuk's electricity needs. A high-voltage power line crosses two fjords to reach the capital. The free span of the power line—length without support—across the Ameralikfjord is 3 miles (5 km) long, the longest in the world.

In a few very protected spots, Greenlanders can grow potatoes, carrots, lettuce, and spinach. This is usually for the farmer's own use rather than for sale. Some farmers grow crops in greenhouses. Importing fresh fruits and vegetables is expensive. People hope that growing crops in greenhouses will be cheaper.

Greenhouses are needed for growing vegetables and fruit.

The Eqi glacier attracts many visitors.

Tourism

Tourism is becoming increasingly important to Greenland's economy. The number of people visiting the country is on the rise—close to thirty thousand every year. The stunning scenery and fascinating history make it appealing to those who can afford the trip. Air Iceland is one of the main airlines flying into Greenland. Plans are to expand the airport at Nuuk so that passengers can fly directly from Europe instead of having to go to Iceland first.

Greenland offers visitors a variety of attractions. Fishing enthusiasts find plenty of good spots. A hotel made of igloos is available for adventuresome tourists at Langerlussuaq. Some visitors take short trips by dogsled. They can even join longer adventures to the Inland Ice sheet.

The Danish government did not allow privately owned businesses to be started in Greenland until 1950. In the 1990s, the Home Rule Government started selling some state-owned businesses to private owners.

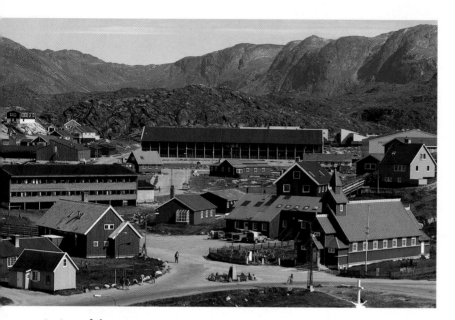

A view of the town of Paamiut on the southwest coast

Greenlanders now run perhaps two thousand small businesses. They are mostly construction companies, small shops, and services for tourists. In 1988, a bottling plant for beer and soft drinks was built in Nuuk.

Private ownership of land is not allowed. Someone needing land to run a business must apply for a government permit to be allowed to use a certain piece of land.

Transportation and Communication

Greenland has fewer than 95 miles (150 km) of roads. None of these roads connect towns. Instead, they are all either within towns or connect to local airports. Only half of these roads are paved. Though Greenland has almost no roads, it has fourteen airports. Nine have paved runways. Almost all transportation in Greenland is either by air or dogsled, although the snowmobile has become popular for short distances.

Greenland's international airport is Kangerlussuaq Airport. It is located north of the Arctic Circle at the end of a long fjord. The airport was originally built in 1941 as a U.S. air base.

Radio broadcasting began in Greenland in 1942. Today, Radio Greenland broadcasts over seventeen radio stations to reach the entire island. Most of the radio broadcasting is done in Greenlandic, one of two official languages. Greenland has only one television station, which broadcasts primarily in Danish, the other official language. Greenland has two national newspapers, *Atuagagdliutit/Grønlandsposten* (meaning "something to read") and *Sermitsiaq*.

Villagers and dogs in Qaanaak Village

Inuit and Dane

W HEN PEOPLE THINK OF GREENLAND, THEY OFTEN THINK of two groups of people, the Inuit and the Danes. But it is not so simple. In many ways, three different groups make up the Inuit in Greenland. The largest group lives in west Greenland and controls much of what happens on the island. Far fewer people live in east Greenland, where they are isolated much of the year in only two towns. The third group, even smaller, is the Polar Eskimos, or Inughuit. These three groups speak different versions of the language and have different ways of living.

Opposite: **A smiling father holds his son.**

Nuuk Inuit gather together.

Inuit and Dane **85**

Persons per square mile	Persons per square kilometer
fewer than 3	fewer than 1
unpopulated	unpopulated

The population of Greenland was estimated in July 2004 at 56,384. About 88 percent of the people were born in Greenland. The remaining 12 percent were born elsewhere, primarily in Denmark.

About one-quarter of the people live in the capital, Nuuk. Most of the rest live in one of the seventeen other municipalities. About ten thousand Greenlanders live in sixty-five little settlements, most of which have fewer than one hundred residents.

In 2004, more than one-fourth of the population was made up of children under the age of fifteen. Less than 6 percent of the people are over the age of sixty-five. The average life expectancy is sixty-nine years.

Health

Historically, the Inuit people were quite healthy. The animals they hunted and fished provided the nutrients they needed. Whale blubber, in particular, contains a lot of vitamin C.

When the Danes took over the island, many Inuit acquired habits that were not as healthy. They caught on to the pleasures of tobacco very quickly. Smoking became a necessity to many Inuit. Today, throat and lung cancer are rampant in Greenland.

Alcoholism and drug addiction are also serious health problems, especially for the young. Many young people feel caught. They have lost the old ways, but they don't have the skills that would allow them to deal with the new world. This same problem means that the suicide rate among young people is very high in Greenland.

Population of Greenland's Largest Towns (2003 est.)	
Nuuk	13,889
Sisimiut	5,222
Ilulissat	4,285
Aasiaat	3,179
Qaqortoq	3,086
Maniitsoq	2,905

The Inuit

Like Native Americans, the Inuit people originated in Siberia, in northern Russia. But the Inuit came to North America many thousands of years after the Native Americans. The ancestors of Native Americans probably walked across a land bridge that existed between Siberia and Alaska during the last ice age. By the time the Inuit came to North America, much of the ice had melted and the seas had risen. The land bridge was now covered with water. So the Inuit's ancestors must have come by boat.

Robert Peary and other explorers noted that the Polar Eskimos were quite short, perhaps an average of

An Inuit mother carries her child in a sealskin amaut.

A Polar Eskimo woman stands beside glacial ice.

only 5 feet (1.5 m) tall. Today, only a few of Greenland's native people are pure Inuit. Most also have Danish ancestry. The group most likely to be pure Inuit are the Polar Eskimos, who were left alone for one hundred years longer than the southern Greenlanders. The average Greenlander is now somewhat taller than his or her ancestors and is just as likely to have curly brown hair as straight black hair.

An Eskimo in New York

In 1897, polar explorer Robert Peary took six Polar Eskimos with him when he left Greenland. He brought them to New York City at the request of the American Museum of Natural History. People at the museum wanted to study "specimens" of Arctic people. All but the youngest, named Minik, soon died. Minik was horrified to discover that his father's skeleton had been put on display in the museum.

After the scientists finished studying Minik, they abandoned him to his own resources in the largest city in the United States. He finally returned to Greenland briefly in 1909, but he had forgotten the language and his hunting skills. He eventually went back to the United States, where he died in the flu epidemic of 1918 at the age of twenty-eight. Minik's story has been exaggerated into many myths told by the Inuit.

The Inughuit

The Inughuit of the north are more closely related to the Inuit of the Hudson Bay area in Canada than they are to Inuit of southern Greenland. The Inughuit are the people most likely to remember the traditional ways of hunting and living.

Hunters search for narwhal in the fjord.

The Inughuit were skilled hunters. Millions of birds nested on cliffs in northern Greenland. The Inughuit not only ate the meat, but also used the skins to sew inner clothing that was worn beneath warm furs. During the spring, when the birds were there nesting, the Inughuit lived among them in tents. They spent the dark winter months in stone huts on the shore.

During the winter, a hunter could get seal by waiting patiently at a hole in the ice for the seal to surface. Then he would kill it with a harpoon. In the spring and summer, the seals would pull themselves through their holes and lie on the surface in the sun. A hunter might spend hours creeping slowly toward the seal so it wouldn't get startled and dive back into the water.

The great prize for Inughuit hunters was a whale. Several people together, including women, hunted from large skin boats called umiaks. Each hunter speared the whale with a harpoon. The whale would struggle to free itself from the harpoon lines, but eventually it would tire. Then the Inughuit could kill it.

Today, the Inughuit still use harpoons and kayaks to get their prey. They look down on the people who come to hunt using powerboats and rifles. In 2004, reporter Maria Cone wrote of the importance of the traditional ways to the northern Inuit: "No factory-engineered fleece compares with the

Harpoon tips used for hunting whales

warmth of a sealskin parka, mittens and boots. No motorboat sneaks up on a whale like a handmade kayak latched together with rope. No snowmobile flexes with the ice like a dog-pulled sledge crafted of driftwood."

But the Inughuit's life is not solely traditional. Life is a mix of old and new. According to journalist Robert Biswas-Diener, "It is a mistake to think of the Inughuit only as traditional hunters. They are, in fact, modern. They drink coffee, surf the Internet, take photos, play soccer, and go to the grocery store. But between playing bingo and broadcasting local radio, they hunt, fish, and carve ivory. . . . They are modern hunters, who have adapted their cultural history to contemporary realities.

A hunter practices throwing a harpoon from his kayak.

Common Greenlandic Words and Phrases

Inuugujaq	Hello
Inuk	Man
Illu	House
Tii	Tea
Anaana	Mother
Ataata	Father
Qujanaq	Thank-you

This stop sign uses both English and Inuit.

It is not uncommon, for example, to find Inughuit parents cutting up whale on the kitchen floor while the children watch the latest Hollywood release on DVD."

The Greenlandic Language

For most of their history, the Inuit did not have a written language. Then about 150 years ago, a missionary named Samuel Kleinschmith developed a way of writing Inuit. The Danes introduced reading and writing into the schools soon after. Today, Greenland has a 93 percent literacy rate.

New Names

Through the 1970s, place names in Greenland were in Danish. But after home rule was established, Greenlanders decided to replace the Danish names with names that reflect features of the place. Here are some examples of name changes:

Frederikshaab became Paamiut, meaning "those at the mouth of the fjord."

Holsteinsborg became Sisimiut, meaning "people at the fox hole place."

Søndre Strømfjord became Kangerlussuaq, meaning "big fjord."

Julianhaab became Qaqortoq, meaning "white place."

Lichtenau became Alluitsoq, meaning "place with few breathing holes for seals."

Sukkertoppen became Maniitsoq, meaning "uneven place."

Kleinschmith's original written version of Greenlandic had many accents. These marks made it look complicated. When Denmark made Greenlandic an official language, it formed a commission to simplify the written language. The commission also designed ways to include words brought in from other languages.

Several Greenlandic words have made it into the English language, though they are spelled differently. *Kayak*, for example, is a small, low boat. In Greenlandic, it is spelled *qajaq*. The Greenlandic name for house is *illu*, which developed into the word *igloo*.

East Greenlandic is quite different from West Greenlandic in both pronunciation and vocabulary. The Inughuit speak yet a different kind of Greenlandic. Many Greenlanders speak English or Danish so they can talk to people outside of Greenland. In fact, most young people speak some English.

Count to Ten in Greenlandic

ataaseq

marluk

pingasut

sisamut

tallimat

arfinillit

arfineq marluk

arfineq pingasut

qulingiluat

qulit

Greenlanders tend to use Danish for numbers higher than ten.

Shamans and Cathedrals

94

THE VERY NAME OF THE ARCTIC PEOPLE STEMS FROM THEIR belief that all living and nonliving things have a soul. They called that soul the *inua*. From that word came the name *Inuit*. The Inuit who came to Greenland call themselves *Kalaaleq*, which means "people with strong shamans."

Historically, the Inuit believed in shamanism. This is a spiritual life based on good and bad spirits interacting in all human affairs and found in all things. A shaman, who might be called a priest, helps people maintain a balance between the good spirits and the bad. These spirits are the spirits of the dead. It is important to maintain a good relationship with the spirits of the dead because they may be helpful to the living.

Opposite: **A hand-carved Inuit wooden figurine**

An Inuit shaman's mask

For the Inuit, shamanism was tightly tied to the hunt. An animal would allow itself to be killed only if the hunter was in harmony with the spirits of the animals. After a successful hunt, the spirits had to be thanked.

In traditional Inuit religion, some gods have names. Sila is the goddess of air and weather. It is important to stay on her good side to maintain a good life above the ground. Sedna, the sea goddess, controls the things of the sea. She gives to the Inuit everything that is good—weapons for hunting, skins to make clothing, blubber to eat and burn in lamps. When Sedna is angry, she gives humans bad things—unsuccessful hunts, severe storms, sickness. It was said that a skilled shaman could fly to the bottom of the sea to visit Sedna.

The Shaman

To become a shaman, a person had to spend long periods fasting, or not eating. This way, the person's spirit was free to acquire knowledge from the invisible. A shaman needed to be skilled on the sacred drum. A steady, beating rhythm on the drum could put a shaman into a trance. Shamans were thought to have special powers while in a trance. They could visit the dead, become invisible, and even fly.

Shamans made and wore small carved figures as their spirit helpers. These figures, called amulets, represented the spirits that were being asked for help.

Tupilak figures are tiny grotesque figures often carved from a whale tooth. To the Inuit of long ago, tupilaks were unseen spirits that shamans used to get rid of an enemy. In 1884, an explorer named Gustav Holm asked the natives what a tupilak looked like. They had never before thought about what a tupilak would look like to other people. They carved a figure to show Holm. This started a new form of art for Greenlanders.

This tupilak depicts a creature with a smug smile and very pointed shoulders.

The Norse and Their Faith

The first Norsemen in Greenland were not Christian. Instead, they worshipped the old Norse gods. Ancient objects showing the hammer of Thor, the Norse god of thunder, have been found in Greenland. During the first hundred years that the Norse were in Greenland, however, they converted to Christianity and built many churches. The Norse left Greenland by 1500, but the ruins of their churches can still be seen today. At its height, the Norse communities had about 300 homes and as many as

Evil Spirits in Nuuk

Shamanism and the belief in evil spirits are not completely things of the past in Greenland. In December 2002, a government employee in Nuuk hired a shaman to "drive away negative energy" from local government offices.

Since most Greenlanders today are Lutheran Christians, many people were offended by this action. Political pressure built up, and eventually, the prime minister was forced to fire the man who had brought in the shaman.

Stories of Light

The aurora borealis, or northern lights, is a phenomenon that occurs in the sky in northern reaches of the world. Many northern peoples have myths that explain the spectacular colors and pulsing, flowing ribbons of light. One Danish legend holds that the lights are caused by the flapping wings of swans that flew too far north and froze. To the ancient Inuit, the lights were an opening onto heaven, where the dead danced. They believed that the shaman controlled the appearance and movement of the lights.

thirty churches. Most impressive is Hvalsey Church, in the old Eastern Settlement.

Norse Greenlanders had their own cathedral with a bishop to rule over their other churches. The island got its first bishop, Arnald, in 1124. Saint Nicholas Cathedral was built in the Eastern Settlement. Little is left of it now.

The Norse in Greenland paid no attention to the Inuit and made no effort to convert them. After the Norse disappeared from Greenland, Christianity also disappeared from Greenland for three hundred years.

The ruins of a Viking church

Missionaries Come to Greenland

By the early 1700s, Denmark controlled Greenland. Denmark had officially become a Lutheran nation in 1536. Lutheranism followed the beliefs of Martin Luther, a German monk who wanted to see reform in the Roman Catholic Church. He became one of the founders of Protestantism.

Leif Eriksson and Christianity

Erik the Red's son, Leif Eriksson (below), traveled to Norway in 999. By that time, the king of Norway had decreed that Christianity would be the national religion in Norway. He persuaded Leif to become Christian,

too. On returning to Greenland, Leif introduced his family to the new religion. Erik refused to give up the old Norse gods, but Leif's mother had a church built. It was the first Christian church built in the New World.

The Apostle of Greenland

Hans Egede (1686–1758) was a Norwegian minister who had studied at the University of Copenhagen in Denmark. He became fascinated by the records of the Norse in Greenland and was determined to visit the country. He was certain that the descendants of the early Norse still lived there. He wanted to bring Lutheranism to them.

Egede and his family led three ships to Greenland. He was disappointed to find no one but the Inuit. He didn't understand them, and they didn't understand him. He decided to do the best he could.

Egede's religion called for a way of life that was very different from the way the Greenlanders lived. Everything they were long used to doing seemed to have become a sin. Egede had a difficult time convincing them to give up shamanism.

The Europeans also brought a deadly disease called smallpox with them when they arrived in Greenland. In 1733, a smallpox epidemic killed most of the native people who lived in Godthaab, the Danish settlement. It also killed Egede's wife. In 1736, Egede gave up and returned to Norway. But his son, Paul, remained in Greenland. Paul had spent most of his life in

Greenland, and he knew the Greenlandic language well. He completed his father's work of translating the Old Testament into Greenlandic.

People in Denmark followed Evangelical Lutheranism. An important part of this religion was bringing the faith to non-Christian people. Hans Egede was a missionary. He both started the Danish settlement of Greenland and began the conversion of the Inuit to Christianity. He eventually became known as the Apostle of Greenland.

Religious Holidays in Greenland

Holy Thursday	Thursday before Easter
Good Friday	Friday before Easter
Easter Sunday	March or April
Christmas Eve	December 24
Christmas Day	December 25

Qaqortoq church from the nineteenth century

Greenland does not have an official church, but almost all Greenlanders are Evangelical Lutherans. Most towns and settlements have a church, which serves as the focus of much of the Greenlanders' lives. An important part of growing up is taking confirmation classes. After a long

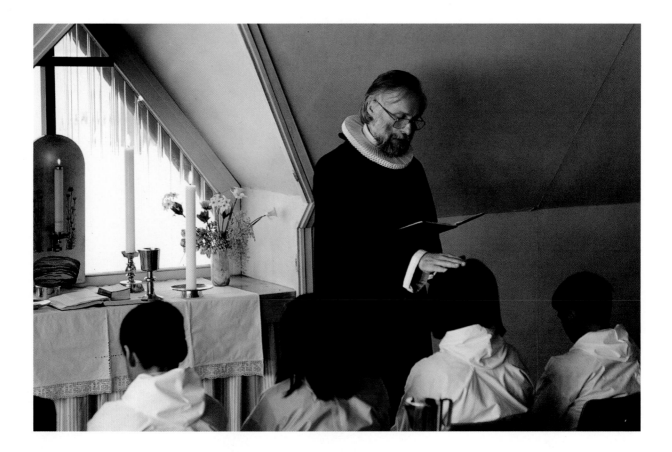

A Lutheran vicar confirms an Inuit youth.

education, a ceremony is held during which the young people are accepted into the church as full adult members.

Many Greenlanders today are committed to bringing back the older cultural life of the island. Much of that life revolved around shamanism and the belief in spirits. Today, Christianity and shamanism sometimes exist side by side. When hunters catch a whale, they may give thanks in a Christian prayer. But the ritual of giving thanks after a successful hunt is ancient. Their ancestors thanked the spirit of the whale for allowing itself to be caught.

Kayaks and Crafts

THE FEW MONTHS OF SUMMER CAN BE A GREAT TIME FOR Greenlanders to celebrate in the outside. Special summer events are often a mixture of sports and arts. Almost every settlement has its museum, its song and drum gathering, or its sporting events.

Opposite: **John Baker-Beall of Australia in action during an ice golf tournament**

An Inuit plays this drum covered with a polar-bear bladder.

Music

The drum dance has been called the only real Inuit form of music. It was originally part of shamanism. In the past, it was also used as entertainment and to taunt enemies. Over the years, the drum dance was almost forgotten. Recently, however, it has been making a comeback. Greenlanders now look to it proudly as part of their heritage. The traditional drum is oval-shaped and covered with a polar-bear bladder.

Much more popular with young people, however, is rock music. Even though Greenland has just a tiny population, it produces an amazing number of recordings that sell widely. The first recording by Greenlanders was made in 1973 by a pop group called Sume, meaning "where." Suddenly, there was a major market for Greenlandic music. In 1976, a nonprofit recording company named Ulo was founded to support Greenland's music, both traditional and pop. Ulo's recording studio is located in Sisimiut.

The Word for Art

The Greenlandic language originally had no word for "art." Greenlanders did not come up with a word for art until Europeans began to pay attention to their work. Then they invented a word that literally means "something odd, which has been constructed." It is *erqumitsufiaq*.

Walrus ivory carvings of an
Inuit scene

Art and Literature

The primary artform of Arctic people has always been carving. They gave fanciful shapes to tools such as harpoons and kayak bows. Even simple household tools were often decorated with tiny figures and drawings. In the twentieth century, skilled artists began to make tupilak figures and other carvings that are now sold around the world.

Aron of Kangeq (1822–1869) is sometimes called the Father of Greenlandic Artists. Aron, who was a seal hunter, may have been taught to draw by missionary Samuel

Kleinschmith. Aron's woodcuts were already famous in Greenland when Dr. Hinrich J. Rink, a Danish natural scientist who studied glaciers, found him. Rink spent his spare time collecting Green-landic folktales, and he asked Aron to do paintings to illustrate them. Though Aron was bedridden with tuberculosis, a severe lung disease, he agreed. The tales and Aron's paintings were published in a now-classic four-volume set called *Legends from Greenland*.

The Katuaq Cultural Center

The Katuaq Cultural Center in Nuuk doesn't just put on exhibits and performances. It also helps performers who want to travel throughout Greenland. This gives the people in even tiny settlements far from Nuuk a chance to see contemporary and classical plays as well as pop music.

Other Greenlandic artists depicted everyday life. A native artist named Gerhard Kleist drew scenes of life on the island in about 1900. A journalist named Hans Lynge (1906–1988) also painted scenes from his native island.

Jens Rosing (1925–) is a renowned historian, archaeologist, and painter. Using watercolors, he illustrated Palle Petersen's 1993 popular children's book of Inuit tales called *Inunguak the Little Greenlander*. Per Danker creates cartoons called *Parca Men*, which make fun of some of the traits of Greenlanders. They are published in the newspaper *Sermitsiaq*.

The first Greenlandic novel was published in 1914. *Sinnattugaq*, by Mathias Storch (1883–1957), was a futuristic story of a young man's dream of Greenland.

Filmmaker Laila Hansen

Film

In 1997, *Heart of Light* became the first full-length movie ever made completely in Greenland. It was also the first film made in the Greenlandic language. Written and directed by a Dane, Jacob Grønlykke, the film deals with the problems of unemployment and alcoholism in Greenland, while incorporating Inuit mythology.

Laila Hansen is an Inuit who has become Greenland's first filmmaker. She directed a 2002 film called *Inuk Woman City Blues*. Hansen is also an actress who has performed throughout the Inuit-speaking areas of Canada as well as in Greenland. She said in an interview: "In the school, they taught us that your heritage is all dead and you only have to see the future. When I became an actress, I toured in small places where people who have never seen (Inuit cultural) theater said, 'They lied to us in school.' They saw that it was alive."

Sports

In Greenland, skiing is a summer sport. In winter, it's just too cold. One summer ski area is near Maniitsoq (the name means "uneven place"), where skiers race down a glacier. The gold-medal-winning Norwegian Olympic team trained there.

The Arctic Circle Race is one of the world's toughest cross-country skiing races. It is held at Sisimiut, 40 miles (65 km) north of the Arctic Circle. The participants travel 100 miles

Cross-country skiing is a popular sport.

Jack O'Keefe of the United States competes in ice golf.

(160 km) in three days over rough terrain and in often terrible March weather. It has been held every year since 1995.

One of Greenland's more unusual sports is ice golf. Ice golf championship tournaments have been held on the glaciers of Uummannaq. The contestants play with orange balls so they'll be able to see them against the white snow.

An Inuit helps launch a friend's kayak.

Soccer, which is known as football throughout most of the world, is immensely popular in Greenland. The first local soccer club was founded in 1933, and the first championships were held in 1958. Today, a national tournament is held in late August and early September. Both adult men and women and junior boys and girls take part. Though almost every little town has a soccer field, people often have to play indoors because it is too cold outside.

Kayaking

The kayaks used by the Inuit on the west coast were specially designed to work in the ice-laden waters of Greenland. They were 17 feet (5 m) long and strong enough to withstand blows by floating ice. They could also be fastened together to make a more stable craft. A different kayak was used on the east coast. It was a two-person craft.

Kayaks were traditionally used for hunting. Today, they are more often used for fun. Sunday afternoons find many Greenlanders out on the fjords in their kayaks. In recent years, almost every community has started a kayak club. Most young people in southern Greenland learn on plastic kayaks.

Kayaking in Disko Bay

Eventually, many will buy kayaks made especially to fit them, or they will make their own.

The Greenland Kayaking Championships are held every year. Maligiaq Padilla is one of Greenland's greatest kayakers. He has traveled around the globe, competing in events and teaching the world about kayaking.

Arctic Olympics

The Arctic Winter Games began in 1970, and they have been held every two years since. Teenage Inuit from Greenland,

An athlete competes in a snowboarding contest.

Alaska, Russia, and Canada take part. The Arctic Games include both regular Olympic sports and traditional Inuit events. The young people compete in alpine skiing, badminton, cross-country skiing, indoor soccer, snowboarding, snowshoeing, table tennis, and volleyball. But they also give their all in events such as the fingerpull, the armpull, the knuckle hop, and long-distance sled hopping.

Other events are not athletic, but they are just as difficult. One such event is throat singing, which is also called overtone singing. In throat singing, the singer makes two tones at once. Traditionally, throat singing was done by women standing facing each other, with one challenging the other to imitate the sounds she makes. The winner is the one who forces the other to stop to take a breath. Truly skilled singers can breathe while singing, so they do not have to stop.

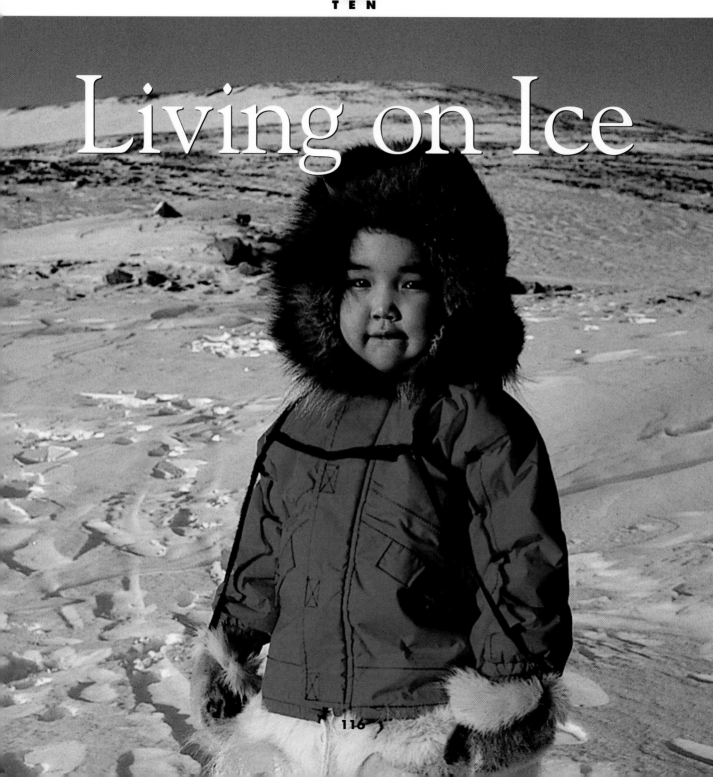

Living on Ice

Most Greenlanders live south of the Arctic Circle on the western side of the island—the protected side. In the summer, the snow melts, and the hills turn green. The lives of people in southern Greenland are much like those of people in other northern countries. People drive to the small shopping malls in Nuuk. School and church events draw family members from a distance. Movies come to town. Children take dance or music lessons. Boys and girls play soccer.

Opposite: **An Inuit girl dressed in traditional winter clothing**

North of the Arctic Circle and on the east coast, things are different. There, life still resembles the way Greenlanders lived long ago. A settlement usually has just one small shop that carries only a few basic items. Bad weather can isolate people for long periods of time. Good medical care may be hard to find, but satellite-powered Internet connections are making the lives of people in these distant areas less isolated.

A market in Greenland

An Inuit puts the finishing touches on an igloo.

Housing

Before the Danes arrived in Greenland, the lives of the Inuit had not changed much for centuries. The people built winter houses of stone and turf. The houses were low, sometimes even dug into the ground, so that winter winds could zoom right across their roofs. People entered the houses through a low tunnel. A single house might be divided up so that several families could live in it.

During the short summers, hunter families were continually on the move, hoping to find enough food to last them through the long winter. They moved from campsite to campsite carrying their possessions, including boats. Summer houses were tents made of two layers of skins. The outer layer was soaked in fat to make it waterproof.

Even south of the Arctic Circle, there was little wood available to build houses. Until the Danes started bringing

Igloos

Traditional Inughuit houses were made of stone and turf. They called these houses igloos. This is their word for any house. What we think of as an igloo—a round structure made of blocks of ice was quickly built only as overnight protection by hunters who then abandoned them as they moved on.

From House to Museum

The oldest wooden house in Greenland is in Qasigiannguit on Disko Bay. It was built in eight days in 1734 by Paul Egede, the son of the first missionary and founder of Nuuk. Today, the house is part of a museum that contains many artifacts returned to Greenland by Denmark.

wood by the shipload to Greenland, permanent houses were made of stone. In places where the land was boggy, houses were often made of peat, pieces of the soil cut into blocks.

Peat is rarely used for building anymore. But a women's organization called *Bedstemorforeningen*, which means "grandma's association," has built a traditional Greenlandic house of peat. The women want to be sure that young Greenlanders know how people lived not very long ago.

This early home was constructed of stone.

Stone huts have not been the main housing since the Danish government started building wooden houses. They are usually identical, which makes small remote villages look oddly alike, except for the variety of colors the residents paint them. These houses are generally perched on rough hillsides, with foundations dug into the slopes around the fjords.

Not many people own their own houses, and no one owns the land their houses stand on since private ownership of land does not exist. Today, the most common type of housing in Greenland is publicly owned buildings where people rent apartments.

There is no privately owned land in Greenland. The buildings pictured here are government-built.

Towns and Schools

Greenland once had more towns than it has now. Most of them had fewer than a hundred people. Towns of that size cannot support the schools and medical clinics that people need. So the Home Rule Government decreed that many of these tiny settlements be shut down and that the people move to larger towns. The number of settlements was cut almost in half. That number has now begun to rise again, however.

Children in Greenland are required to go to school for at least nine years. The courses are taught in Greenlandic. Most secondary schools are directed toward specific trades so that young people can find jobs. A young person who attends secondary school can study areas such as building, metalwork, foods, animal husbandry, fishing, and laboratory technical work. Greenland's only folk high school is located in Sisimiut. The folk school is uniquely Nordic. Students are taught more for cultural enrichment than for professional training. Called Knud Rasmussen College, the school, which opened in 1962, has worked to conserve the Inuit culture and strengthen the students' understanding of themselves as Inuit.

Greenland also has general education high schools at Nuuk, Qaqortoq, Aasiaat, and Sisimiut. Greenland is working

An Inuit teacher works with her students.

toward being able to keep the graduates of these high schools in Greenland for higher education. The University of Greenland is located in Nuuk. In 2003, it had 100 students and a staff of 21. It offers a three-year bachelor's degree, plus a two-year master's degree. Among the subjects taught are public administration, cultural and social history, Greenlandic language and literature, and theology.

The University of Greenland is a member of the University of the Arctic, which includes institutions from Lapland, Alaska, and northern Norway. Among its subjects is circumpolar studies.

Greenland also has a college called the Seminary. It offers a four-year program that trains primary school teachers. It also trains social workers.

Boats are the main source of transportation in Greenland.

Traveling

The main way of getting around Greenland is by boat. Boats travel up and down the coast, as long as the harbors aren't frozen. Anyone going north of the open harbors has to take an airplane or helicopter, which is expensive. There are only a few cars in Greenland because there are only a few roads. Nuuk has streets and even parking lots. At the airport in Kangerlussuaq, roads lead to the hotels.

Snowmobiles, also called snowscooters, are an increasingly popular form of transportation south of the Arctic Circle. They are frowned upon for long journeys, however. They disturb wildlife, make noise, and can be dangerous if someone runs out of fuel or spills out far from help. But they are being used for short trips to fishing sites, to run errands, or for just plain fun.

In the north and along the east coast, the dogsled is still the primary means of transportation. The center of the dogsledding area is the town of Ilulissat, where there are more dogs than people. It has been said that a Greenlander must hunt for twice as much food as he needs to feed his family because he also needs to feed his dogs.

Because a good dog team can mean the difference between life and death, the dogs get special protection. Though they generally live out in the cold, they may be allowed into the tunnel leading to a winter house during severe storms. The dogs wear small skin boots when they need to run on rough ice.

An Inuit man trains his huskies.

Throughout most of the Arctic, sled dogs are in pairs when they are in their harnesses. But that arrangement can be dangerous in Greenland. The snow may hide pits or crevasses. If the front pair of dogs falls into a crevasse, they could pull the entire team and the sled in with them. For safety, then, in Greenland all the dogs in a team generally run side by side. That way, if one dog falls, the others probably will not follow.

Holidays

With the arrival of Christianity in Greenland, Christmas became an important holiday. Christmas occurs during the polar winter, when the sun never rises. Because of this, light is an important part of the celebration in Greenland. Town Christmas trees and lights in every house window are seen from the beginning of Advent (the fourth Sunday before Christmas) until Mitaartut (Epiphany), which is January 6. In recent years, Greenlanders have begun to include the Swedish tradition of a Saint Lucia procession in their Christmas activities. On January 6, children dress in disguise and make all the noise they want.

New Year's is celebrated with fireworks at two different times. First they are set off at 8 P.M., which is midnight in Denmark. Then more fireworks are set off at midnight, Greenland time.

The National Day

Greenland's National Day is June 21, which is the longest day of the year. It is called *Ullortuneq*, which means "the longest day." Because the sun never sets on this day, there's plenty of time for celebration. Picnics, entertainment, and parties are held throughout the day while the Greenland flag flutters everywhere.

The Anorak

The traditional jacket of the east Greenlander is the anorak. These warm jackets are pulled on over the head and reach below the hips. Anoraks were first made of caribou, seal, or even bird skin. After the arrival of the Danes, they began to be made of cloth. Today, an anorak may have a zipper down the front.

Clothing and Food

The traditional clothing of the Inuit was made from the animals they hunted—seals, polar bears, caribou. The clothing was warm because they wore skins with the fur side inside. Air would be trapped in the spaces between the hairs and warmed by the body.

This Greenlander still needs a sweater in the summer.

Men who hunted on water needed waterproof clothing. Women made the clothing. They made an inner layer of warm skin. This was covered by an outer layer of sealskin, which is naturally waterproof.

The need for warmth hasn't changed. But in towns, almost everyone now wears clothing such as blue jeans and sweatshirts. Even on the warmest summer days, a sweater or jacket is usually necessary. Special occasions, such as Sundays and holidays, will bring out the traditional clothing.

Women's traditional dress clothing consists of a brightly colored, hand-knit sweater, fur shorts, and tall, white fur-lined sealskin boots. The sewing of the boots and the embroidered tops reflect the woman's creativity.

This woman wears the traditional beaded costume of Greenland.

The hunters of Greenland were very smart when it came to mittens. Like all clothing, they were made of skin, but the traditional mittens had two thumbs. That way, it didn't matter which hand a mitten was thrust into.

In the past, whale was the most important prey for Inuit hunters. When hunters were lucky enough to get a whale, the luck belonged to the whole community. They all shared in the work of removing the blubber. While they worked, bits of blubber were cooked to snack on. The whole community also shared the food and oil removed from the animal. Today, whales and other large animals are hunted only in the northern communities. Most northerners live on seal about half the year. A dogsled team also requires a seal every two days for the energy to do their work.

Greenlanders in the south are more likely to eat fish and shrimp. They also eat caribou, which has usually been grown on a caribou farm.

Inuit String Figures

The Inuit used to spend their long dark winters doing whatever they could to help pass the time. One of the skilled arts the women developed was making figures from string. This was a little bit like our game of cat-in-the-cradle, but the figures were much more complex. Some Inuit can make a loon, a child sledding, or a seal resting on ice. Children, especially girls, start learning to make the traditional figures at about age five.

Old and New

Greenland is a fascinating mix of old and new, north and south, ice and land, and relaxed and difficult living. The people who arrived there from across the Arctic long ago established a way of life that worked well in the icy world they found. Today, the outer world is finding the Inuit, and the Inuit are wholeheartedly embracing the outer world.

The task of Greenlanders now is to keep what has worked for them in the past and mix in the best of what the new world offers. Together, this combination can build Greenland's future.

Young girls on the docks of Ilulissat harbor

Timeline

Greenland History		World History	
The first people arrive in Greenland.	**ca. 2500** B.C.	**2500** B.C.	Egyptians build the Pyramids and the Sphinx in Giza.
The Saqqaq people settle in southern Greenland.	**1400** B.C.		
		563 B.C.	The Buddha is born in India.
		A.D. **313**	The Roman emperor Constantine recognizes Christianity.
		610	The Prophet Muhammad begins preaching a new religion called Islam.
The Thule culture arrives in Greenland from Alaska.	A.D. **900s**		
Viking Gunnbjørn Ulfsson is the first European to see Greenland.	**ca. 930**		
Erik the Red settles in Greenland.	**982**		
Erik the Red leads a major settlement to Greenland.	**986**		
Thorvald, Erik the Red's son, makes first contact between Europeans and Native Americans in North America, in what is now Canada.	**1004**		
		1054	The Eastern (Orthodox) and Western (Roman) Churches break apart.
		1066	William the Conqueror defeats the English in the Battle of Hastings.
		1095	Pope Urban II proclaims the First Crusade.
		1215	King John seals the Magna Carta.
The Norse settlers in Greenland accept rule by the king of Norway.	**1261**	**1300s**	The Renaissance begins in Italy.
		1347	The Black Death sweeps through Europe.
		1453	Ottoman Turks capture Constantinople, conquering the Byzantine Empire.
The Norse settlement in Greenland ends.	**ca. 1480**	**1492**	Columbus arrives in North America.
		1500s	The Reformation leads to the birth of Protestantism.

Greenland History		World History	
A missionary named Hans Egede settles near what is now Nuuk, beginning Danish settlement.	1721		
The Royal Greenlandic Trade Company is established.	1776	1776	The Declaration of Independence is signed.
		1789	The French Revolution begins.
Captain John Ross meets the Polar Eskimos in northern Greenland.	1818	1865	The American Civil War ends.
American Robert Peary likely becomes the first person to reach the North Pole.	1909	1914	World War I breaks out.
		1917	The Bolshevik Revolution brings communism to Russia.
		1929	Worldwide economic depression begins.
		1939	World War II begins, following the German invasion of Poland.
		1945	World War II ends.
The United States establishes an air base at Thule.	1951		
Greenlanders becomes full citizens of Denmark.	1953	1957	The Vietnam War starts.
An American B-52 bomber carrying nuclear weapons crashes near Thule.	1968	1969	Humans land on the moon.
		1975	The Vietnam War ends.
Home Rule is introduced.	1979	1979	Soviet Union invades Afghanistan.
		1983	Drought and famine in Africa.
		1989	The Berlin Wall is torn down, as communism crumbles in Eastern Europe.
The first Nuuk Marathon is held; in 2003, the name is changed to the Arctic Marathon.	1991	1991	Soviet Union breaks into separate states.
		1992	Bill Clinton is elected U.S. president.
		2000	George W. Bush is elected U.S. president.
		2001	Terrorists attack World Trade Towers, New York and the Pentagon, Washington, D.C.

Fast Facts

Official name: Kalaallit Nunaat ("Land of the People")

Capital: Nuuk

Official languages: Greenlandic, Danish

Jakobshavn, named for Jakob Severin

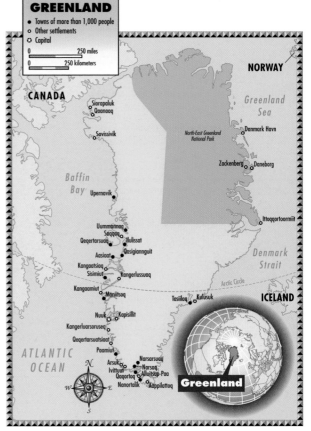

Greenland's flag

Kayaking on
Kangerlussuaq Fjord

Official religion:	None
Year of founding:	Home Rule Government approved 1979
National anthem:	"Nunarput Utpqqarsiammgpravot" ("You Our Ancient Land")
Government:	Parliamentary democracy within a constitutional monarchy
Chief of state:	monarch of Denmark
Head of government:	prime minister
Area:	839,999 square miles (2,175,597 sq km); 668,000 square miles (1,730,000 sq km) is ice cap
Distance north to south:	1,660 miles (2,670 km)
Distance east to west:	652 miles (1,050 km)
Borders:	Arctic Sea, Greenland Sea, Denmark Strait, Labrador Sea, Baffin Bay
Coastline:	24,396 miles (44,087 km)
Highest elevation:	Gunnbjørn, 12,139 feet (3,702 m)
Lowest elevation:	sea level
Average temperature in the south:	21°F (−6°C) in winter; 45°F (7°C) in summer
Average temperature in the north:	−31°F (−35°C) in winter; 39°F (3.6°C) in summer
Average precipitation:	14 inches (35 cm) per year

Dog sledding

Danish kroner

National population (2004):	56,384	
Population of largest towns (2004):	Nuuk	13,889
	Sisimiut	5,222
	Ilulissat	4,285
	Aasiaat	3,179
	Qaqortoq	3,086
	Maniitsoq	2,905

Industry: The largest percentage of the population works in public administration. The primary industry is fishing, especially shrimp. Greenland is economically supported by Denmark.

Currency: Danish kroner

System of weights and measures: metric

Literacy rate: about 93 percent

Common Greenlandic words and phrases:

Inuugujaq	Hello
Inuk	Man
Qajaq	Kayak
Illu	House
Tii	Tea
Anaana	Mother
Ataata	Father
Qujanaq	Thank-you

An Inuit girl

Knud Rasmussen

Famous people in Greenland's history:

Aron of Kangeq *Called The Father of Greenlandic Artists*	(1822–1869)
Hans Egede *Missionary who resettled Greenland after the Vikings disappeared*	(1686–1758)
Leif Eriksson *Erik the Red's son; led an expedition to mainland North America*	(ca. 970–1020)
Matthew Henson *Explorer who worked with Robert Peary*	(1866–1955)
Samuel Kleinschmith *Missionary who established the written Greenlandic language*	(1814–1886)
Robert Peary *Leader of probably the first expedition to reach the North Pole*	(1855–1920)
Knud Rasmussen *Inuit-Dane who studied the Inuit throughout the Arctic*	(1879–1933)
Erik Thorvaldsson (Erik the Red) *Viking who encouraged people in Iceland to settle Greenland*	(10th century)

To Find Out More

Books

▶ Buell, Janet. *Greenland Mummies*. Millbrook, Conn.: 21st Century Books, 1998.

▶ Harper, Kenn. *Give Me My Father's Body: The Life of Minik, The New York Eskimo*. Hanover, N.H.: Steerforth Press, 2000.

▶ Howarth, David. *The Sledge Patrol: A WWII Epic of Escape, Survival, and Victory*. New York: The Lyons Press, 2001.

▶ Love, Ann, and Jane Drake. *The Kids Book of the Far North*. Toronto: Kids Can Press, 2000.

▶ Malaurie, Jean. *Ultima Thule: Explorers and Natives in the Polar North*. Translated by Willard Wood and Anthony Roberts. New York: W. W. Norton & Co., 2002.

Videos and DVDs

▶ *Globe Trekker—Iceland and Greenland*. 555 Productions, 2004.

▶ *Iceland and Greenland*. Lonely Planet, 1997.

▶ *Nova: B-29 Frozen in Time*. PBS, 1996.

▶ *Nova: The Vikings*. PBS, 2000.

Web Sites

▶ **Greenland: Land of Ice and Snow**
http://www.wbur.org/special/
dispatches/greenland/dispatches/
*An environmental reporter's
photographic expedition to Greenland.
The site also contains multimedia files,
including a chance to hear a young boy
speak Greenlandic.*

▶ **Inuit Circumpolar Conference**
www.inuit.org
*The official Web site of the Inuit
Circumpolar Conference.*

▶ **Greenland Tourism**
www.greenland.com
*This site contains all kinds of
information about visiting Greenland.*

▶ **Greenland Research Centre at the
National Museum of Denmark**
http://www.sila.dk/
*This site provides a cultural history
of Greenland.*

Index

Page numbers in *italics* indicate illustrations.

Meet the Author

Jean F. Blashfield delights in learning lots of fascinating things about places and the people who live in them. She says that when writing a book for young people, she's often as challenged by what to leave out of the book as what to put in. She has long been intrigued by the Vikings, the Arctic, and people who live in out-of-the-way places. Greenland fits all those categories.

She has been a traveler since she first went on a college choir tour of Europe and made up her mind that she would go back. After developing the *Young People's Science Encyclopedia* for Children's Press, she kept that promise to herself and returned to London to live. That city became her headquarters for three years of travel throughout Europe. It was in London that she first began to write books for young people.

Since then, she has returned to Europe often (but not often enough, she says!), while writing a hundred books, most of them for young people. Her favorite subject is interesting

places, but she loves history and science, too. She has created
an encyclopedia of aviation and space, written popular books
on murderers and house plants, and had a lot of fun creating a
book on women's exploits called *Hellraisers, Heroines, and
Holy Women.*

Jean Blashfield was born in Madison, Wisconsin, and cur-
rently lives in Delavan. She graduated from the University of
Michigan and worked for publishers in Chicago and
Washington, D.C. But she returned to the Lake Geneva area
in southern Wisconsin when she married Wallace Black, a
publisher, writer, and pilot. She has two grown children, two
cats, and two computers. In addition to researching via her
computers, she produces whole books on the computer, scan-
ning pictures, creating layouts, and even making the index.
She has become an avid Internet surfer and is working on her
own Web site, but she'll never give up her trips to the library
or to other countries.

Photo Credits

CONTENTS

The Charm Bracelet

Copyright © 2000 by Emily Rodda

www.harperchildrens.com

Library of Congress Cataloging-in-Publication Data
Rodda, Emily.
  The charm bracelet / Emily Rodda. — 1st American ed.
    p.   cm. — (Fairy realm ; #1)
  Originally published: Sydney, N.S.W. : ABC Books, 2000.
  Summary: When Jessie searches for her ill grandmother's missing
charm bracelet, she is led to a magical world and finds she has a reason
and right to be there.
  ISBN 0-06-009583-0 — ISBN 0-06-009584-9 (lib. bdg.)
  [1. Grandmothers—Fiction.   2. Fairies—Fiction.   3. Bracelets—
Fiction. 4. Fantasy.] I. Title.
PZ7.R5996 Ch 2003   2002017276
[Fic]—dc21   CIP
                                                                 AC

Typography by Karin Paprocki
7   8   9   10
❖
First American Edition
Previously published by ABC Books for the
AUSTRALIAN BROADCASTING CORPORATION
GPO Box 9994 Sydney NSW 2001
*Originally published under the name
Mary-Anne Dickinson as the Storytelling Charms Series 1994*

Fairy Realm

BOOK 1

The Charm Bracelet

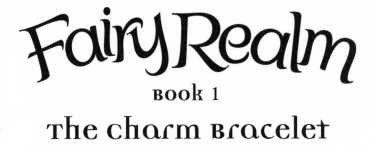

EMILY RODDA

ILLUSTRATIONS BY RAOUL VITALE

HARPERCOLLINS*PUBLISHERS*

Fairy Realm

Book 1

The Charm Bracelet

FAIRY REALM

The Flower Fairies

The Third Wish

ROWAN OF RIN

Rowan of Rin

Rowan and the Travelers

Rowan and the Keeper of the Crystal

Rowan and the Zebak

Rowan of the Bukshah

CHAPTER ONE

The secret garden

Jessie felt better once she was in the secret garden. She sat down right in the center of its smooth, small square of lawn and looked around.

Yes, here at least nothing at all had changed. This place still made her feel as safe and peaceful as it always had. Clustered around the edges of the lawn, her grandmother's favorite spiky gray rosemary bushes still filled the air with their sweet, tangy smell. Behind them the tall, clipped hedge still rose high on every side. When Jessie was little, she used to think the hedge made this part of her grandmother's garden very special. Its wall of leaves

1

seemed to keep the whole world out.

But, thought Jessie, clasping her hands around her knees, it doesn't keep the world out. Not really. The secret garden's just a place at the bottom of Granny's real garden. It's a place where I can be alone for a while, and pretend things are still the way they were before Granny fell and sprained her wrist. Before Mum started worrying about Granny living alone, and decided she *must*, absolutely must, move out of Blue Moon, her big old house in the mountains, and come to live with us.

She remembered the last time she and her mother, Rosemary, had come to stay with Granny. It had been winter, nearly three months ago. There had been no talk of Granny moving then. Then, things had been very different.

Jessie had always loved winter at Blue Moon. Every evening, as it got dark, they would light a fire in the living room, and then Jessie and her mother would sit cuddled up on the big squashy chairs watching the flames while Granny made dinner.

"No, I don't want help. You sit down and rest,

Rosemary," Granny would say to Mum. "You work too hard. Let me look after you—just while you're here. I love to do it." And after a few minutes' protest, Mum would agree, and settle back gratefully, smiling.

Then for a while the only sounds they would hear would be the popping and snapping of the fire, the purring of Granny's big ginger cat, Flynn, crouched on a rug, and Granny's voice as she moved around the kitchen, singing the sweet songs that Jessie remembered from when she was a baby. There was one song that she had always especially loved. *Blue Moon floating, mermaids singing, elves and pixies, tiny horses* . . . it began. Jessie thought Granny had probably made it up, because it didn't rhyme, and the tune was lilting and strange.

Inside Blue Moon it was warm, cozy and safe. Outside, huge trees stretched bare branches to a cold black sky that blazed with stars, and in the morning a dusting of white frost crackled under your feet when you walked on the grass.

It had always seemed strange and magical to

3

Jessie. At home there were no big trees and no frost. And the city lights seemed to drown the brightness of the stars.

But if winter in the mountains was magical, spring was even better. In spring everything sparkled. The bare trees began to bud with new leaves of palest green, and in their shade bluebells and snowdrops clustered. Bees buzzed around the lilac bushes that bent their sweet, heavy heads beside the house. Butterflies of every color and size danced among the apple blossom. In spring it was as if Blue Moon was waking up after a long sleep. Everywhere there were new beginnings.

But not this spring, Jessie thought sadly. This spring was more like an ending. She'd been feeling sad ever since her mother had told her about the plan to take Granny home with them at the end of this visit.

"Don't you want Granny to live with us, Jessie?" her mother had finally asked her, as they drove up the winding road that led from the city to the mountains. "You two have always been so close, especially since your dad died. I

4

thought you'd love the idea."

Jessie tried to explain. "It's just that . . . I can't really imagine Granny away from Blue Moon," she said. She turned her head away, pretending to look out the window, but really not wanting her mother to see the tears she could feel prickling in her eyes. "And . . . I'll miss . . . coming up here," she burst out. "I'll miss the house, and the trees, and the secret garden."

"Oh, darling, of course you will!" Mum took one hand off the steering wheel to stroke Jessie's long red hair. "So will I. Blue Moon's my old home, remember. I love it, just like you do. But Jessie, it's been five years since Grandpa died. And you know how worried I've been about Granny living all alone without anyone to look after her." She smiled. "My dad might have been the artist in the family, but he was a very practical man all the same. You wouldn't remember, I suppose. But he was sensible, and took no risks. Which is more than you can say for Granny, bless her heart."

Jessie in fact did remember Grandpa quite well, even though she'd been so young when he died. His name was Robert Belairs. His paintings had been sold all over the world and were in many books. But to Jessie he was just Grandpa, a tall, gentle man with kind blue-gray eyes, a short white beard and a beautiful smile. She remembered how he always let her watch him paint in his upstairs studio at Blue Moon. And she remembered the paintings he worked on there—the soft, misty mountain landscapes, and the fairyland scenes for which he'd become so famous.

It was the fairy pictures that Jessie had especially loved. Sitting quietly on a stool beside him, she used to watch with wonder as a fantasy world came to life under her grandfather's brush, a mysterious and beautiful world full of golden light. Lots of these paintings hung on the walls of Blue Moon, because every year, on Granny's birthday, Grandpa had painted a special picture just for her. He'd finished the last one just before he died.

Robert Belairs' fairyland was a world of pretty cottages, treehouses and shining castles, and elfin-faced people in wonderful floating clothes. He always called these people "the Folk." The most beautiful and royal-looking of the women had long golden-red hair and green eyes like Jessie's own. This had pleased her very much, though she knew that Grandpa wasn't really painting her. He'd always painted his fairy princesses that way. People used to laugh and say that was why he'd fallen in love with her grandmother in the first place. Granny's hair was white now, of course, but when she had first come to Blue Moon to marry Robert Belairs her hair had been as red as Jessie's.

Grandpa's paintings were also full of busy gnomes, dwarfs, pixies and elves, thin little brownies, and tiny flower and rainbow fairies with gossamer wings. There were sometimes miniature horses, too, their manes threaded with ribbons and tiny bells. Jessie had really loved those. She had thought her grandfather was very clever to be able to paint such pictures. Maybe he was a bit magical himself.

And yes, she remembered how carefully he had looked after Granny, too. When Mum and Jessie had visited Blue Moon in those days, it was Granny who cooked the delicious food they ate, who talked

7

and laughed, who suggested all sorts of outings and adventures and never expected anything to go wrong. But it was Grandpa who packed the extra box of matches for the picnic, "just in case." It was Grandpa who took the umbrella when they went on a walk, "just in case." It was Grandpa who made sure there were spare keys to all the doors, "just in case."

Granny used to tease him about it. She'd reach up to pat his cheek, the gold charm bracelet she always wore jingling on her wrist. "You always expect the worst, Robert. Don't worry so. All will be well," she'd say. And he'd smile, and touch her hand. "Better to be safe than sorry, princess," he'd answer. And quite often he was right.

Jessie could understand why Mum thought Granny couldn't exist safely without him. But she just knew Mum was wrong. Her mind went back to the argument they'd had in the car on the way up to Blue Moon.

"Granny tripped over that stray kitten that came in!" she'd protested. "That had nothing to do with being alone, Mum. That could happen to anyone, any time. And she only sprained her wrist."

"But Jessie, it could have been so much worse!" Her mother had frowned. "If she'd hurt her leg or something she could have lain there in pain for days without being able to call for help." Her hands had tightened on the steering wheel. "You have to be sensible about this, Jessie," she'd said firmly. "And so does Granny. Both of you have to listen to me for a change. What's needed round here is a bit of common sense!"

Now, sitting in the secret garden, Jessie realized that her mother was really very like Grandpa. She had his kind blue-gray eyes and his strong practical streak. She wasn't like Granny at all. But Jessie was. She knew that quite well. For one thing, she looked like Granny. She was going to be taller, of course: that was obvious, since already they were about the same height. Jessie wore an old gray cloak of Granny's for a dressing gown when she came to stay at Blue Moon, and even when she was in bare feet it didn't trail on the ground.

It was from Granny that Jessie had inherited her red hair, green eyes and pointed chin. She had been named Jessica after Granny, too. But, more important than name or looks, Jessie and her grandmother shared a love of stories, songs and fantasy that made them really enjoy each other's company.

And there was something else. They simply understood each other. Jessie always knew how Granny was feeling about things, and Granny always knew how Jessie was feeling, too. It had been like that ever since Jessie could remember.

Was that why, when Jessie had run into Granny's bedroom after they'd arrived at Blue Moon an hour ago, she had immediately felt so worried and sad? Was that why she hadn't been able to bear staying there, but had had to escape to the secret garden? Was that why . . . ?

Jessie sat perfectly still. Without warning, a thought had whirled into her mind. She began to shiver, her eyes wide and startled, her hands gripping the soft grass. Suddenly she had become terribly sure of something. Granny was in trouble. Real trouble. It wasn't just a matter of a sprained wrist, or sadness, or loneliness. It was something far more dangerous.

She sprang to her feet. She didn't know where the thought had come from. But now it was there, she knew it was true. And she had to do something about it. She didn't know what. But she had to help. She had to!

She began running for the house.

CHAPTER TWO

The Missing Bracelet

At her grandmother's bedroom door Jessie hesitated. Her heart was thumping. She smoothed her tangled hair and tried to calm down. Mum and Nurse Allie would still be with Granny. They'd be alarmed if she burst into the room in a panic.

She felt the soft tap of a paw on her ankle, gasped with fright, and looked down to meet the solemn golden eyes of Flynn, her grandmother's cat. He had been sitting so quietly in the dim hallway that she hadn't noticed him. She crouched to stroke his soft fur.

"Are you keeping guard on Granny's door, Flynn?" she asked him. "Won't Nurse Allie let you inside?"

He stared at her, unblinking.

"She would, you know, if only you wouldn't fight with the gray kitten," Jessie whispered, moving her hand around to scratch him under the chin. "It wasn't the kitten's fault that Granny fell, you know, Flynn. It was an accident."

Flynn rumbled in his throat, a noise more like a growl than a purr.

"Don't worry," Jessie soothed him. "Granny will be feeling better soon. Nurse Allie's going home now that we're here. Mum's a nurse, too, and Granny will be quite all right with her. So tonight I'll let you into Granny's room. The kitten can stay out, for a change. Everything's going to be all right, Flynn."

But when she opened the door and slipped into the bedroom, she wasn't so sure. When they'd first arrived, Granny had been sitting in her comfortable chair by the window. Now she was lying in bed, looking pale and ill. Rosemary was sitting beside her, hands clasped on the flowery bedcover, while in the corner of the room Nurse Allie, plump and busy, measured out medicine. The little gray kitten, Flynn's enemy, purred softly on the window seat.

Granny's long white hair, braided into a thick plait, trailed over the pillows. One wrist was heavily bandaged. The bandage was much more obvious now that she was lying down and her arm was out of the sling she'd been wearing earlier.

She smiled faintly at Jessie. "Where have you been, Jessie?" she asked. Even her voice sounded different. It seemed to have lost its music.

"I've been to the secret garden," Jessie said, moving over to stand beside the bed.

Granny smiled again. "Oh, yes," she murmured. "The secret garden. You love it, don't you, Jessie?"

"Maybe you could come there with me, tomorrow morning," Jessie suggested eagerly, taking her hand.

"Well, that might be a little difficult for Granny, dear," beamed Nurse Allie, bringing the medicine over to the bed. "But you could sit out on the front verandah for a while, Mrs. Belairs, couldn't you? The fresh air would do you the world of good. Cheer you up!"

"We'll see," said Granny softly. "I just feel . . . so tired." Her eyelids fluttered closed.

Jessie looked despairingly around the room. Why was Granny like this? She saw that Nurse Allie was shaking her head at Mum in disappointment. Cheerful Nurse Allie, with her crisp curls and smart uniform, had tried very hard to make things pleasant for Granny while she waited for Mum and Jessie to come.

She'd used every trick she knew to brighten up the bedroom. She'd brought in vases of spring flowers. She'd opened the curtains to let in the sunshine. She'd let the gray kitten play on the rug. She'd noticed that the dark, mysterious painting on the wall facing the bed, the last painting Grandpa had done before he died, made Granny cry, so she'd taken it away and put a pretty mountain scene in its place.

But nothing had worked. Granny lay quiet and

16

listless in her bed, or sat obediently in her chair, without showing any sign of cheering up or getting well.

Jessie was still for a moment. Then she noticed something. She stared. Why hadn't she noticed this before?

"Granny, where's your bracelet?" she asked. Never before had she seen Granny without her gold bracelet, so thickly hung with charms that it tinkled on her wrist with every movement.

The old woman's eyelids slowly opened. "Bracelet?" she mumbled. She looked confused, and then there was a flash of memory and panic in her eyes. Her fingers tightened on Jessie's hand. "It's lost!" she muttered. "Jessie . . . it's gone. They . . . must have taken it off while they were fixing my wrist." She struggled to rise from her pillow. "Jessie, you must find it for me. You must! I need it!"

"Now, now, don't let's get ourselves into a froth!" crooned Nurse Allie, frowning at Jessie. She pressed Granny gently back on to the pillows. "Now, we've been through all this, dear. We know the bracelet must be somewhere, don't we? It's quite safe. It's been put away in some drawer or other, that's all."

"I must have it!" protested Granny, moving her head restlessly.

"You just concentrate on getting better, Mum," said Rosemary. "We'll worry about the bracelet later."

"But time is running out! It's nearly my seventieth birthday!" Granny cried. Then she stopped, and a strange, puzzled expression crossed her face. "My birthday? Why does that matter?" she whispered.

Nurse Allie stepped forward briskly. "A little rest is what you need, I think, dear," she said, shooting a warning look at Rosemary and Jessie. "All this excitement! Goodness me!"

"Sorry, Nurse," said Rosemary. She stood up and pushed Jessie a little crossly to the door. Jessie could see there was no point in arguing. Both Mum and Nurse Allie thought she was making Granny upset. She let herself be ushered from the room.

Flynn looked at Jessie and her mother with

wide eyes as they closed the door softly behind them, but he made no move to follow them out to the back of the house. He just settled back to his guard duty, still as a statue, in the dim hallway.

"Jessie, you mustn't worry Granny," Rosemary said sternly as they reached the kitchen. "Not about the charm bracelet, or the secret garden, or anything. She's not well. She has to have peace and quiet." She began pulling things out of cupboards, getting ready to start dinner. Then she turned around and tried to smile.

"Look, darling, don't worry too much," she said. "It's only natural for Granny to be depressed. Just think about it. Her wrist must be very sore. And it's her birthday the day after tomorrow. It wasn't long after her birthday five years ago that Grandpa died. It makes her sad to think about it."

"But Mum . . ." Jessie looked at her mother's kind, worried face and thought better of what she'd been about to say. Mum wouldn't understand about the feeling of danger she'd had in the secret garden. And she wouldn't understand why

19

she felt the charm bracelet was so important. After all, Jessie didn't really understand it herself!

All Jessie knew was that Granny was in trouble. And that the charm bracelet she always wore was missing. And that for some reason the bracelet had to be found before Granny's birthday the day after tomorrow. Jessie clenched her fists. She made herself a promise that she would find the bracelet if she had to look behind every cushion and in every drawer in the house to do it! After dinner she'd check Granny's room. Then she'd do the living room and the kitchen. She'd be sure to find it before bedtime.

But bedtime came and still the bracelet had not been found.

Jessie lay cuddled up in bed in the small room that was always hers at Blue Moon and thought hard. Of course there were many more places she could look. But she couldn't see how the bracelet could have got into one of the spare rooms, for example, or the dining room, or the sunroom either.

She closed her eyes. The bed was warm and

soft, and the sheets smelled faintly of rosemary. She was very tired. Her thoughts began to drift. In the morning she'd try again. In the morning . . .

Her eyes flew open again. She could have sworn she'd heard a very faint tinkling sound. It sounded just like the charm bracelet when it jingled on Granny's wrist. And it had come from outside, in the garden. She was sure of it.

She threw back the covers, jumped out of bed and ran to the window. Outside, grass and flowers shone in the moonlight. The trees held their budding branches up to the sky, throwing deep shadows on the lawn. Jessie strained her eyes, but there was nothing more to be seen. Nothing but the gray kitten, slinking through the trees toward the secret garden.

Jessie shivered. She left the window and ran back to bed, jumping in and pulling the covers tightly around her. There was no one out there. She must have imagined the sound. She closed her eyes again and tried not to think about the bracelet. Again the warmth of the bed stole around her. Then, suddenly, she thought of a place she hadn't looked. When Nurse Allie had taken Grandpa's painting off Granny's bedroom wall, she'd put it in his studio for safekeeping. Jessie heard her tell Mum so. Maybe she'd absent-mindedly put the bracelet there, too.

The more Jessie thought about it, the more likely it seemed. The studio. First thing in the morning, she'd look there. With a sigh of relief she turned on her side, and in a few moments was asleep.